JOHN

Discovering
Period Gardens

SHIRE PUBLICATIONS LTD

Contents

Cover photograph: *Stourhead landscape garden.*

ACKNOWLEDGEMENTS
Illustrations are acknowledged as follows: John Anthony, 1, 4, 6, 10, 21-2, 29, 30-3, 35-6, 38-9, 48-9, 52-3, 61, 63, 69-71; Cement and Concrete Association, 50; Department of the Environment, 15; Cadbury Lamb, cover photograph, 2, 3, 9, 11-14, 17-20, 24-6, 28, 30, 34, 37, 40-1, 43-7, 51, 54-9, 62, 64-8; National Gallery, 27; National Trust for Scotland, 8; Shakespeare Birthplace Trust, 7; Provost and Fellows of Worcester College, Oxford, 5.

British Library Cataloguing in Publication Data: Anthony, John. Discovering Period Gardens. – 4 Rev. ed. – (Discovering Books; No. 129). I. Title. II. Series. 712.60941. ISBN 0-7478-0340-4.

Published in 1997 by Shire Publications Ltd, Cromwell House, Church Street, Princes Risborough, Buckinghamshire HP27 9AA, UK.

Printed in Great Britain by CIT Printing Services, Press Buildings, Merlins Bridge, Haverfordwest, Pembrokeshire SA61 1XF.

1
Early gardens

Gardens are as old as civilisation. Ever since man ceased his wanderings as a nomad and settled down to live in a fixed place he has sought to arrange the immediate surroundings of his dwelling place in a way which satisfies his needs and desires of the moment. Thus the earliest gardens came into being.

A garden is a partnership between man and nature with, generally speaking, man having the upper hand over nature. It is a controlled piece of nature; nature tamed and adapted to human needs.

Most gardens are essentially settings to buildings, usually a dwelling, ranging from palace to cottage. The design of buildings varies from age to age and is indeed one of the principal signs of the thought and manners of the age which built it. Similarly gardens vary in design as one age succeeds another; partly as a reflection of architectural design, but also in relation to changing concepts of man's relationship to his natural environment.

Roman gardens

The first people to make gardens in Britain were probably the Romans. We have little real information as to what these gardens were like beyond the fact that there were gardens. The typical larger house plan was quadrangular with a garden in the centre and really large houses would have a series of these quadrangles each with its own garden. Remains of pools and fountains have been found and there were elaborate pavements with designs and pictures set out in variously coloured tesserae. Whilst distantly related to the gardens of the opulent villas of Roman Italy, they were much smaller, but perhaps quite well related to the very different climate.

The Romans introduced numerous trees and plants to this country, many of which survived the subsequent near extinction of civilisation. Fruit trees and culinary vegetables seem to have been extensively cultivated. Even the vine was imported from the shores of the Mediterranean and, after some difficulty, acclimatised.

Medieval gardens

The gentle art of gardening can only flourish in settled, civilised conditions and it was not until well into the middle ages that gardens became at all common or important features. These seem to have been of two main kinds.

Monks were the earliest medieval gardeners. The customary plan of a monastery was a rectangular arrangement of buildings around a cloistered quadrangle. The space within the quadrangle seems always to have been very simply treated with grass and was

1. A medieval walled garden of the late fifteenth century.

frequently the burial ground of the community. The monastery garden proper was usually associated with the infirmary buildings, for one of the most important functions of the garden was to supply not only food but also the herbs upon which medieval medicine so largely depended. In at least some of the monastic orders provision of flowers for the decoration of the numerous altars was a hardly less important function of the garden. The layout of these gardens must have been of the simplest kind and would seem decidedly utilitarian to our eyes.

Castle gardens originated with the rough courtyards within the walls which in early times must have been as decorative as a farmyard and not dissimilar in use. Rising living standards led to the creation of small ornamental gardens within part of the space inside the walls. Judging from illustrations in illuminated manuscripts of the time these gardens were often formed of a network of paths between which were raised beds planted with flowers. Curious features, which occur repeatedly, are the seats of turf with flowers growing in the grass — not perhaps very serviceable in a typical damp English summer. A mound seems to have been a common feature and from the top one could look out beyond the walls to the countryside around. But castle gardens can never have been nearly as impressive as monastic ones for they had to be fitted in among the defences, and space must always have been restricted.

By the fourteenth century more settled conditions led to the build-

2. *The mount, complete with somewhat utilitarian arbour, within the garden at Boscobel House, Shropshire. The house is famed as the hiding place of Charles II after his defeat at the Battle of Worcester in 1651 but the garden is of interest quite apart from the replanted oak within which Charles took sanctuary.*

3. *The turf seat raised on a low wall and a timber arched arbour at Queen Eleanor's Garden at Winchester. Although confined to a very small area and hemmed in by surrounding buildings the garden shows a variety of features typical of a medieval garden.*

4. *Queen Eleanor's Garden at Winchester Castle. The garden is named after the wives of Henry III and Edward I who both spent much time at the castle. The plants are all ones with which they would have been familiar.*

ing of less heavily fortified houses. Here it was possible to provide a garden on a more ample scale, although they still seem to have been of quite moderate size. An enclosing wall or wattle fence of woven osier was provided, or perhaps it might be a hedge of thorn or later of box, privet or yew. Around this enclosure there would be an earthen mound with low retaining walls of stone or timber. One side of the garden would sometimes be formed by a side of the house with an entrance from the lord's solar or withdrawing room. A second gate into the enclosure enabled the gardeners to have access without coming into contact with the lord and his family and guests.

Raised beds of flowers, often with trees, occupied some of the space within, but the greater part would be simply rough grass on which the ancestors of modern ball games might be played. Bowls and tennis had their origins in this way. Grass cutting was unknown and the only maintenance possible was by returfing the area every few years. Covered walks and arbours with trellis work of light timber make their appearance towards the end of the period, perhaps providing a degree of privacy in the garden which was lacking in the houses of the time.

Tudor gardens

With the coming of the Tudors and the ending of the upheavals of the Wars of the Roses the arts of peace could flourish as never before and among these that of garden design began to develop.

Monastic gardens had long since lost their importance and the dissolution of the monasteries meant but little loss to gardening. The rich noblemen no longer needed to live in fortresses and were able either to adapt their castles into more comfortable and expansive houses or, more commonly, to build new, purely domestic and unfortified houses. In either case there was much more scope for the gardens now considered essential. This increasing emphasis on domesticity was further reinforced by the emergence of the rising classes of new noblemen and landed gentry, who often obtained possession of former monastic lands and buildings.

Tudor gardens are directly descended from medieval ones and, especially in the time of the early Tudor monarchs, retained most of their medieval features but on a more ample scale. Gradually the new ideas in art and architecture emanating from Italy and called by us the Renaissance, began to influence ideas on the design of buildings and, rather later, on those of gardens.

Renaissance influence can be felt in much greater regularity in the arrangement of the parts of the garden, with beds disposed about an axis which would often be designed to relate to the main axis of the facade of the house, thus bringing the two into a formal rela-

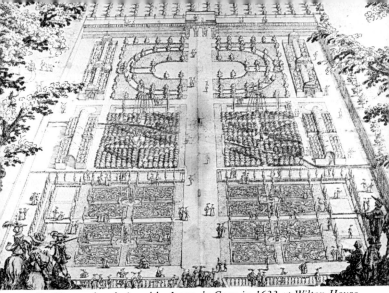

5. *The garden designed by Isaac de Caus in 1633 at Wilton House, Wiltshire, the first fully Italianate garden to be made in England. Although it straddled the river Nadder the design ignores this awkwardness in its strict formality.*

tionship which would have been meaningless to medieval man.

Trees were gradually banished beyond the confines of the garden into the deer parks, which now usually lay just outside. Walls of stone or brick were likely to take the place of the medieval hedges or wattle fences but the raised walks and mounts continued to be an important feature. Ascended by a spiral path, the mount would now be topped by a small garden-house of timber, replacing the leafy arbour of former times. Similarly the raised walk would now be embellished by a stone balustrade of somewhat classical design in the new mode. Here the owner might sit and contemplate the deer in his new park or view the extent of his estates round about.

No Tudor garden remains intact, but features of some have been preserved. There are many written accounts of the gardens of the period and from these we have an impression of increasing complexity. A taste developed for wooden ornamental rails and small carved statues painted in bright colours. Sundials of a number of complex types were a frequent feature and the age was one of much activity on the purely horticultural side of gardening.

In place of the raised beds of medieval times, which were designed to be seen at close quarters, a distinctively Tudor feature evolved — the knot garden, which was intended to be seen from a distance and from the higher level of the terrace or the mound. Knot gardens consisted of a rectangular arrangement of beds, each compartment being filled by an intricate geometrical design. These designs were carried out in box or other shrubs, closely clipped into a low hedge. Sometimes herbs such as thrift were used for this purpose and infillings included flowers, low-growing shrubs and coloured gravels. Knot gardens had the advantage of retaining almost their full effect during winter but required an inordinate degree of maintenance by hordes of painstaking gardeners. Time has not, therefore, been kind to knot gardens but there are a number reconstructed on more or less authentic lines.

From the complexities of the knot garden it is but a small step to the maze. This was known long before the Tudors but first makes its appearance as a popular garden feature at this time. The design would be simply marked out in low shrubs, the hedged maze, more properly called a labyrinth, being a rather later development. The well known maze at Hampton Court is of this latter type, although

6. The garden of the Tudor House Museum, Southampton, designed to display the features and planting typical of the late Tudor period. It is one of the best and most authentic modern garden reconstructions.

it originated in an older one.

The early Tudors tended to regard flowers as so much material with which to fill the spaces of the knot garden. But later came the publication of the earliest books on plants, known as herbals, those of Gerard and Parkinson being especially famous. Many new plants were introduced such as the carnation and the gilly-flower, ancestors respectively of our pinks and wallflowers. In the kitchen garden cabbages, the pale gooseberry and the apricot arrived. Other plants, previously rare, were now cultivated in quite modest gardens, among them strawberries and raspberries.

The beginnings of the science of botany can be ascribed to this time and the period is also notable for the frequent use of floral motifs in architectural decoration. Many a newly rich Elizabethan, when he had his portrait painted, chose to face posterity with a flower in his hand.

During the long reign of Elizabeth I the main lines of the Tudor garden continued to form the basis of design but flowers come to hold a more important place than formerly. The increasing wealth

7. The garden at New Place, Stratford-upon-Avon, the home of Shakespeare in retirement. This is an early twentieth-century reconstruction of a sixteenth-century knot garden on part of the site of the garden that existed in Shakespeare's day.

8. A detail of one of the parterres of the Great Garden at Pitmedden, Grampian, where the National Trust for Scotland has reconstructed the formal garden first laid out by Sir Alexander Seton during the late sixteenth century.

and self-confidence, which is so outstanding a feature of the age, led to the building of great country houses surrounded by vast parks. The gardens of these houses were but larger versions of the contemporary type — a series of gardens divided by walls and raised walkways and containing a variety of knots diversified with fountains, fishponds and other water features.

9. *The garden before the Old Palace at Hatfield House, Hertfordshire. Recent replanting and restoration of the several formal gardens have been designed to retain the seventeenth-century atmosphere.*

10. *The fountain garden at Haddon Hall, Derbyshire, forms part of the terraced gardens created during the seventeenth century. Prior to early twentieth-century restoration, during which the pool and fountain were added, this was a simple lawn below the windows of the long gallery.*

2
Stuart and early Georgian gardens

In the seventeenth century England was very receptive to new gardening ideas from abroad and the new plants arriving from overseas. During the greater part of the century French influence was paramount; later, ideas from Holland became the dominant influence.

The nature of French gardens stems from the rather flat, large-scale landscape of much of northern France. Once released from the bounds set by medieval requirements of defence, French gardens expanded to cover vast areas. Great breadth and strict symmetry are the outstanding features of French gardens of the time.

The great expanse of such a garden needed some dominating motif to hold the design together and this was supplied by very strongly emphasised axes to the design. From the centre of the symmetrical facade of the house was set out the dominant axis, either side of which identical features balanced each other. Cross axes would be set out, each of these with symmetrical features either side. There was much use of water — formal rectangular expanses of water to add the reflection of the sky to the colour values of the garden.

The sides of the garden were strongly defined by masses of trees arranged to provide the sharpest possible definition to the enclosure thus provided. The main axis might be further emphasised by parallel alleyways of pleached trees such as limes. There were few changes of level and terraces and mounds were quite alien to the style. These gardens were then divided up into rectangular sections, as in the case of the Tudor gardens, although the scale was generally much larger. The term *parterre* is applied to these sections and they were set out with designs in box or yew filled with smaller shrubs, flowers and coloured earths or gravels. Obviously they were derived from the earlier knot gardens but the patterns were usually much larger in scale and more free-flowing in design.

The great practitioner in this style of garden design was Andre Le Notre, gardener to Louis XIV, who developed it to its limits. Versailles is his greatest work but hardly less important are Fountainbleau and Saint Cloud. French gardeners of this period were the envy of Europe and every monarch of any pretension at all tried to create his own Versailles usually, of necessity, much reduced in scale.

Beyond the garden the main lines of the layout projected out into the surrounding woods to form the basis of another layout of intersecting *allées* or avenues stretching across the landscape.

In England, although French ideas were dominant for the greater part of the seventeenth century, the English distaste for carrying anything to its logical conclusion resulted in many modifications to the style. English noblemen were unable, or at least unwilling, to spend the vast sums required to carry out such schemes on the greatest scale. Moreover, for the full effect a reasonably flat site was required so that the eye would carry along the great vistas. Such sites were rare in the English countryside.

The influence of Le Notre in England increased after the Restoration. Earlier it had been represented by the work of two French designers, Isaac and Soloman de Caus who were responsible for gardens made at Hatfield and Wilton. The gardens have long since gone but records show that, although French in symmetry and of greater breadth of scale than Tudor gardens, they were of rather modest dimensions compared with their counterparts across the Channel.

After the Restoration the full extent of French influence was evident. More French designers worked in England and English designers visited France. Although there is a longstanding tradition that Le Notre himself visited England there is no real evidence that he ever did so, although he may have supplied drawings for some English gardens. Most of these French-style gardens

11. At Edzell Castle, Tayside, the parterre planting has been restored within the enclosing walls of the early seventeenth-century pleasance.

12. The Queen's Garden within the Royal Botanic Gardens, Kew. Based upon the style of c. 1630, the garden was laid out in 1969 between the house known as Kew Palace and the Thames.

13. The restored seventeenth-century gardens at Ham House, Richmond, Surrey, where the National Trust has recreated the layout of 1671-93. The formal garden to the east of the house is shown here but there is also a wilderness and lawns divided by gravel walks in authentic manner.

14. At the Queen's Garden at Kew there is a mount with a wrought-iron arbour on top reached by a spiral path through clipped box. From the arbour one may look over the garden or outwards over the wall to the Thames. The mount was made by reshaping and covering with soil a large heap of boiler-house ashes.

15. The maze at Hampton Court Palace is the earliest hedge maze in England and survives from the Wilderness which was planted c.1690. In subsequent replanting the original hornbeam has been replaced by yew.

have since disappeared due either to neglect or, more commonly, to developments in a later mode.

Foremost among English practitioners in the French manner were George London (?-1714) and Henry Wise (1653-1738). Their special gift was to select and adapt the style so that gardens of rather modest dimensions might yet seem to be in a fashionable style. In 1681 London founded Brompton Park Nurseries on the site now occupied by the South Kensington museums. Six years later he was joined by Wise. London appears to have been the designer, travelling immense distances on horseback to visit clients, whilst Wise managed the nurseries and superintended the Royal gardens at Hampton Court, Kensington, St James's and Windsor. They were the first to grasp the usefulness of a service of advice on the design of gardens and the value of a large nursery able to supply plants as required anywhere in the country.

The Dutch garden

Following the accession of William and Mary in 1688 Dutch influence tended to replace that of France as the keynote of English garden design. The flatness of Holland meant that gardens there

16. Elaborate designs of Dutch parterres, seventeenth century.

had to be on a single level, and thus reinforced the French tendency for gardens to be quite flat. In Holland canals were necessary for drainage purposes and were exploited as attractive features of their gardens. So in England greater use of sheets of water is apparent at the close of the seventeenth century.

Dutch influence also led to a tendency to concentrate on elaborate detail and the scale was much reduced from that of the French manner. There was a profusion of statues, now in lead, trees planted in tubs so that they could be moved about, and box hedges in intricate designs. Bulbs become common in gardens during this phase, the vogue for planting tulips developing into a veritable mania for a time.

Topiary, the clipping of shrubs into artificial shapes, is especially characteristic of this period, although the practice really goes back to the Romans. Topiary was extremely popular in Holland at this time and was eventually carried to ridiculous lengths. From simple geometric shapes such as cones and pyramids, the enthusiastic clippers produced birds, men, wild animals and even corkscrews. Earlier topiarists had usually favoured rosemary but box, whitethorn, privet and juniper were also used. Yew, the commonest shrub nowadays for this purpose, was brought into favour only

18

17. *Westbury Court, Gloucestershire. The formal water garden was constructed between 1696 and 1714 and carefully restored after acquisition by the National Trust in 1967.*

18. *The gateway in the seventeenth-century walls surrounding the main garden at Packwood. To either side of the gate-piers can be seen some of the arched recesses for bee-hives beneath the raised walk.*

19. The well known yew garden at Packwood House, Warwickshire, is said to represent the Sermon on the Mount. The main planting of the yews was carried out in 1850, despite being frequently dated to the seventeenth century.

from the mid seventeenth century. The outstanding topiary garden is that at Levens Hall in Cumbria where the great clipped trees have reached gigantic sizes and quite dominate the garden.

Plants and planters

The seventeenth century was a period of great horticultural activity. John Rose (1629-77) studied under Le Notre at Versailles and became gardener to Charles II at St James's. While undoubtedly a considerable designer, he is remembered today chiefly as a gardener, one of the earliest men to make a name for himself as such. His skill as a vine grower was especially remarked upon by his contemporaries.

This was a period, too, when many plants from overseas were first introduced into this country. Holland was the premier trading nation and England had especially close ties with the Dutch. Through Dutch merchants came plants from both the East and the West Indies, South America and many Mediterranean countries.

Trees were a subject of particular interest from the mid seventeenth century. Much of this was due to John Evelyn (1620-1706), who in 1664 published his *Sylva*, a book advocating the widespread planting of forest trees. He also did much to popularise the newly introduced species and generally aroused a widespread interest in trees.

Shrubs grown purely for their foliage were popular and were known as 'greens', the commonest being mock orange. Often they were planted in tubs and set out in the garden in summer. In the winter they were brought indoors into a 'greenhouse', hence the modern name for a glasshouse. Gardeners were slow to realise the importance of maximum light for plant growth and seventeenth-century greenhouses usually had a tiled roof or even an upper storey where the gardener lived. Nurserymen began to be of some standing in society and several quite large firms grew up.

The systematic study of plants really began in the seventeenth century with the founding of the Oxford Botanic Garden in 1621. This was a simple rectangular layout with cruciform paths surrounded by a wall with three imposing gateways. Physic gardens served the rather different purpose of providing herbs for medicinal use. The Chelsea Physic Garden dates from 1673 and one founded in Edinburgh about the same time was destined to become the Royal Botanic Garden, Edinburgh.

20. *Powis Castle, near Welshpool, Powys. The spectacular terraces below the castle are believed to date from the close of the seventeenth century or the very early eighteenth century. The terraces once overlooked a baroque garden but the profusion of sculpture and planting remains notable.*

21. *Hardwick Hall, Derbyshire, retains the early seventeenth-century garden walls within which the National Trust has laid out this herb garden with plants grown in the seventeenth century.*

3
The English landscape garden

During the early years of the eighteenth century there was a gradual realisation that the formal garden inspired by French and Dutch influences had been carried about as far as it could be. This feeling was at first confined to very few, for the most part writers rather than designers or gardeners, and perhaps reflected a tiredness with well drilled rows of little clipped shrubs and the tidiness of the parterres. Foremost among these writers were Joseph Addison (1672-1719) and Alexander Pope (1688-1744), the latter satirising bitterly the crudities of the formal garden when carried to extremes. Instead of formality they felt that nature, or their conception of nature, should be the guide.

The results of this literary activity in terms of actual gardens were at first very tentative. In an otherwise axial and perfectly formal layout some of the paths in out-of-the-way parts of the garden would wind in a curious way. A 'rectangular' sheet of water would have sides of a serpentine curve rather than merely straight. Pope's own garden at his villa at Twickenham was of this type but has now all but disappeared.

Charles Bridgeman (?-1738) was the earliest garden designer to advance towards the new informal style and he succeeded Henry Wise as Royal Gardener. His manner is not really all that different from that of his predecessor but he sometimes varied the formality of his layouts by introducing the occasional informal touch.

The garden of Chiswick House is today one of the few places where this tentative approach to a more informal type of design can be seen. The garden was planned around a villa built in the latest Italian style by Lord Burlington and dates from the 1720s. The layout is based upon a series of vistas planned as formally as any of the seventeenth-century gardens. A series of temples, obelisks and other architectural features is arranged to provide focal points to be seen at the ends of these glades, but some are also intended to be come upon by the visitor in a less obvious way, from oblique angles. Some pathways wander seemingly at will and, perhaps most prophetically of all, the villa itself is seen from some angles beyond a clear expanse of turf instead of across the customary elaborate parterres.

Chiswick House owed much to its owner, but the design of the garden was the work of William Kent (1685-1748). Of humble origins, he worked as a painter before turning his hand to landscape design and architecture. After feeling his way at Chiswick his later work was much more naturalistic, using the 'ha-ha' to make the turf of the park appear to come right up to the walls of the house. The

22. The 'ha-ha' is a concealed ditch which prevents animals from straying into the garden while at the same time creating the illusion of an uninterrupted sward between the house and the more distant landscape.

ha-ha consists simply of a ditch around the garden area immediately about the house. The side of the ditch nearest the house is constructed as a near vertical stone or brick retaining wall, the other side sloping down gently from the park. Cattle and sheep grazing in the park were thus prevented from coming inconveniently close to the house, but without any barrier being seen from the house.

23. Designs for 'Small Gardens and Parterres for the Town' from 'The Theory and Practice of Gardening', a translation by John James of a work by Alexander Le Blond, published in 1728.

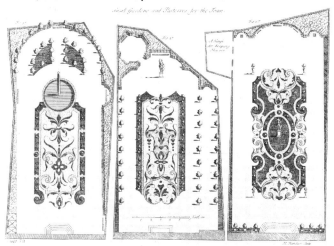

24. The garden at Rousham House, Oxfordshire, was one of the earliest landscape gardens and was adapted by William Kent from an earlier layout by Charles Bridgeman. The statue of Venus is here seen contemplating the landscape of her vale, an incident of the carefully contrived route through the garden.

This very simple idea is important not so much in itself as for what it made possible, for the aim of the designers of this new school was to create a garden which would be an idealised version of nature herself. Thus the whole landscape, and not just that part of it within the garden boundaries, became the garden. This attitude to the landscape is the exact antithesis to that of medieval man, who saw the landscape beyond the garden boundaries as a wild and hostile world and wanted his garden to be as strong a contrast as possible to this. Eighteenth-century men looked at the landscape around the garden and sought to 'borrow' it and bring it within the garden; indeed to make the garden part of it.

25. *The pavilion at Wrest Park, Bedfordshire, was designed by Thomas Archer and built between 1709 and 1711 to provide a focal point for the view from the house down the long canal. Inside, on the principal floor, is a stately domed room with painted walls, whilst below there are servants' rooms and a kitchen.*

26. *The formal garden at Wilton was swept away between 1732 and 1738 by the ninth Earl of Pembroke and replaced with a landscape garden embellished by this Palladian bridge, designed by the Earl and Roger Morris.*

27. 'The Marriage of Isaac and Rebekah' by Claude. Idealistic land-scapes such as this, painted in Italy during the seventeenth century, were an important stimulus in the evolution of the landscape gardens of the eighteenth century.

Landscapes in paint

This wholly new attitude to garden design was much influenced by the landscape of Italy seen by English noblemen on the Grand Tour, which was becoming a conventional feature of their education about this time. In Italy they saw a rocky, wild and romantic landscape with which they had been familiarised by the work of certain French artists, mostly of the seventeenth century, who worked in Italy and painted the landscape. The most important, Claude Gelee (1600-82), known as Claude Lorrain or simply Claude, portrayed a vision of the landscape of Italy in classical times. His pictures are constructed on well defined lines, with trees at the sides framing the view rather like the wings of the stage in a theatre. The clear foreground leads the eye to the centre of the composition. Ruined buildings are disposed on vantage points in the hilly landscape which, however rocky, is always liberally provided with trees. To the forester many of the trees may appear ill-grown but they merge the better into the picture. Often in the middle there is a sheet of water winding away into the distance to meet the golden glow which seems to illuminate the entire scene.

Probably one corner contains several figures which serve to emphasise scale and provide occasion for the title.

Gaspard Dughet (1615-75), sometimes referred to as Gaspard Poussin, also painted landscapes of this type which were hardly less influential than those of Claude. Salvator Rosa (1615-73) invested his pictures with a barbaric quality and a delight in the severity of a landscape of rocks and crags which is quite alien to that of Claude. The figures are often those of banditti, which were felt to be particularly redolent of that most eighteenth century of emotions, the sublime.

It is significant that these painters came into vogue as portrayers of the ideal landscape half a century or more after their deaths. The sons of the English nobility bought their canvasses in Rome and took them back to their estates in England, where today they may still be seen on the walls of country-house drawing-rooms, while through the windows one can gaze on the landscape in which they attempted to create, with English turf, trees, landform and buildings, that ideal landscape which had been composed on canvas.

28. Studley Royal, North Yorkshire: the 'green' garden laid out in the valley of the River Skell from 1716 to 1781. The geometrically-shaped water features are designed to reflect garden temples and other buildings.

29. *The Temple of Music at West Wycombe Park, Buckinghamshire, stands on an island in Swan Lake formed, like the cascade, by damming the River Wye. This landscape garden was one of the most admired when it was completed in the mid eighteenth century.*

'Capability' Brown

So great a change in the practice of gardening on the grand scale raised many difficulties in practice. Fortunately the hour called forth the man and Launcelot Brown (1716-83), always known by his nickname of 'Capability', was on hand to supervise the transformation. His nickname arose from the frequency with which he advised landowners that their property had great capabilities for improvement. Born of humble parentage in Northumberland he moved south to Wootton in Buckinghamshire in 1739 and, a year later, to Stowe in the same county, where William Kent was then carrying out alterations in the new manner to the layout which had been designed not many years previously by Bridgeman. By the time of Kent's death in 1748 Brown had so far progressed from his original menial station that he was placed in charge of the work, which soon attracted attention. He began to advise other landowners and in 1751 he moved to London and set up in practice as landscape architect.

30. Stowe, Buckinghamshire. All the leading landscape designers of the eighteenth century made their distinctive contribution to this great landscape garden. Here the Temple of British Worthies is seen across the stream in the Elysian Fields, which were designed by William Kent to resemble a classical paradise and laid out during the 1730s.

Brown has often been criticised for reducing garden design to a set of rules. Certainly there are some distinctive features which mark his work. The edge of the park is defined by thick belts of trees, usually beech. Within, the natural features of the site are skilfully adapted to create a smooth rolling effect, with a lake of serpentine outline in the middle distance before the house. The turf, gently rising and falling right up to the house, is set off by clumps of trees, usually beech, but sometimes oak or chestnut, especially near the house. The whole effect is one of serene grandeur.

Brown had to cover such long distances to inspect far-flung sites, meet his patrons and supervise operations, that it would be surprising if his work did not vary in quality, and some certainly is rather perfunctory and repetitive. But at his best he could rise to heights which are still the envy of his professional successors. The list of his works is long but Longleat, Harewood, Heveningham, Burghley and Petworth are especially fine. Undoubtedly his masterwork is Blenheim Park where landscape design is carried to a height of perfection it has rarely achieved.

31. *Petworth, West Sussex, where 'Capability' Brown landscaped the park for the second Lord Egremont under contracts dated between 1753 and 1756. The house is seen beyond the lake created by Brown in the middle distance of the views across the park.*

32. *Sheringham Hall, Norfolk, one of the finest of the landscape parks of Humphry Repton. The house, also by Repton, was built for Abbot Upcher in 1812 and, although near the sea, faces inland for protection from storms.*

Brown has often been blamed as the destroyer of the fine formal gardens which often preceded his works and indeed there are many we would willingly give much to see again. But to be denied the experience of seeing his superb parks would surely be too high a price to pay. He rose to be on familiar terms with the great, who hesitated to reject the advice of one so eminent in his field. He was Royal Gardener to George III and amassed a modest fortune with which he purchased a small estate at Fenstanton in Huntingdonshire without, however, adding any sort of park for himself there. In the church he lies buried with his family.

Repton and the Picturesque

After Brown the leading landscape designer was Humphry Repton (1752-1818). He was of the gentry of Norfolk and in 1788, finding himself in reduced circumstances, he set up as a 'landscape gardener', the first to use the term. He already had extensive connections with potential aristocratic clients and with these he rapidly developed a practice almost on the scale of Brown's.

33. *Chatsworth, Derbyshire, where the park designed by 'Capability' Brown replaced a strongly formal layout. The River Derwent, which flows through the park, is made to play its part in the scheme by being dammed to look like a narrow lake.*

A distinguishing characteristic of a Repton design is reduced size, for the great age of vast, sweeping parkland was on the way out. Then the plantations become thicker and the trees larger, with a much greater variety of trees planted. But the greatest contrast of all is to be found in the immediate surroundings of the house. Brown always sought to have the house rise sheer from the turf of the park. This was never very convenient for the occupants but such was the character and influence of Brown that they put up with it. Repton was altogether more accommodating, usually providing at least a gravelled walk before the principal windows, if not a terrace with balustrade as well. Somewhere near the house he would often include what was termed a 'pleasure garden', a small scale layout of paths between lavish plantings of shrubs and flowers. At the end of his life interest in the newly introduced flowers was such that the flower garden returned to fashion after an absence of almost a century. In unfashionable gardens — and there were many — it had, of course, never really been absent.

Repton was a skilled professional man. He drew up a 'Red Book', a report for his client, illustrated with excellent water colours with folding slips of paper to show the view before and after carrying out his proposals. The Red Books are still prized possessions in the libraries of some of the houses where he was called upon for his services.

The period when Repton was in his prime was that when a feeling for the 'picturesque' was felt to be the best basis for landscape design. The origins of the picturesque movement are complex and its progenitors felt it necessary to vilify Capability Brown and even Repton. Their main point was that each part of a layout should constitute a picture which would produce in the mind of the observer certain emotional responses of the kind which are normally associated with painting. Repton replied on his own behalf and Brown's but today the arguments seem particularly remote and tedious. Repton was, in any case, much affected by picturesque ideas himself.

The picturesque school of design placed much emphasis on the right buildings being used at suitable points to create appropriate atmosphere. Ruined buildings were felt to be especially evocative of the right kind of emotions. Suitable ruins were naturally rather scarce but there was nothing to prevent new ruins being specially built. Thus one end of a ruined Gothic castle might in reality be a cowshed artfully disguised. The taste for grottoes, caves lined with shells or rockwork, was also characteristic of the period. For the full effect one really needed an aged retainer living as a hermit in the grotto to give a suitably picturesque feeling to the scene.

The landscape of movement

These landscape gardens or parks were meant to be appreciated by an observer on the move, probably in a coach and four. Today a motor-car driven at a moderate speed will do equally well. The formal garden is one to walk about in, to pause and look along the vistas and absorb the effects which the designer has arranged. In a landscape garden the observer is presented with views which gradually merge into one another. There are no fixed points where one should stop to admire the view.

The speed of movement of the observer for which the layout is designed varies in different gardens and sometimes in different parts of the same garden. Some of the early landscape gardens were obviously designed with the pedestrian in mind. The garden at Rousham House in Oxfordshire, by William Kent, is quite small but the visitor passes along a well defined route experiencing a series of varied scenic effects designed to make the most of the modest beauties of the valley-side site and the surrounding landscape. Stourhead in Wiltshire has a landscape garden quite di-

34. The Gothic Watch Cottage beside the lake at Stourhead, Wiltshire. This was not a feature originally intended by the second Henry Hoare when he created his 'enchanted' lake in the mid eighteenth century but was one of the additions made by his grandson in the early years of the nineteenth century when the vogue for rustic structures was at its height.

35. *The formal gardens at Castle Howard, North Yorkshire, were created in the nineteenth century within the vast eighteenth-century landscape garden with its lakes, temples and mausoleum.*

vorced from the house and comprising an artificial lake in an encircling vale around which a path takes the visitor through a carefully calculated series of visual experiences, with the aid of a series of distinguished architectural features. Notwithstanding these early exceptions, most landscape gardens are much broader in scale and better geared to the movement of carriage or motor-car rather than of pedestrian.

36. *The formal gardens at Belton House, Lincolnshire, were created in the late nineteenth century to replace part of the eighteenth-century landscape garden which had in turn replaced elaborate formal gardens. The Camellia House seen here was designed by Wyattville and built in 1823.*

37. *Trentham Gardens, Staffordshire: the formal gardens created during the 1830s and 1840s by Sir Charles Barry and W. A. Nesfield. Although the house was demolished in 1911 the gardens have long been a popular attraction.*

4
Victorian gardens

By the 1830s the landscape garden had begun to seem dull and insipid. The far corners of the world were being ransacked for floral treasures and in a landscape garden these were necessarily consigned to the kitchen garden or other enclosed, subsidiary space where their bright colours would not disrupt the parkland with its carefully modulated colour scheme of greens, greys and browns. Garden owners now desired some style of garden which would enable them to display their flowers as prominently as possible.

In artistic matters the nineteenth century was a time of looking back, however much scientific and industrial matters had advanced. The taste of the day was satisfied by looking back to the gardens of Italy during the Renaissance. These gardens had a rectangular, geometric form which accorded particular prominence to the terrace, well adapted to the hilly sites common in Italy but less satisfactory in English conditions. Nevertheless the new style of gardening developed with all the easily recognisable features of such gardens: elaborate, if low, balustrades to the terraces, prominent statuary and fountains, and strongly axial layouts. The parterres returned to the garden but with all the gaudy colours of greenhouse exotics lavished upon them which no Italian of the Renaissance would have recognised. This was done by rearing plants in the greenhouse and planting them out in beds in spring. Only low-growing plants were usually used and these were confined by pinching out any shoots which had the temerity to grow above their fellows. Very elaborate designs could be set out in this way and the plants available by this time enabled a virtually unlimited range of colours to be employed.

Loudon and the Gardenesque

J. C. Loudon (1783-1843) was among that large body of distinguished gardeners who were born in Scotland but found fame south of the border. A man of varied interests, his importance lies mainly in his writings, both in books and in the several periodicals he founded and edited, in which he stressed the contribution which scientific method could make to gardening.

Loudon designed few gardens himself and of these little is left today. The main exception is Derby Arboretum which can claim to be the earliest purpose-designed public park, opened in 1840. This is appropriate, for Loudon was much interested in the movement for creating public parks for the rapidly growing industrial towns of the nineteenth century. At Derby he had a long, narrow flat site on what was then the edge of the town. This he varied by artificial hillocks which form sinuous shapes just high enough to separate the area visually into distinct parts. On the sides of these hillocks the botanical kingdom was displayed and labelled as a sort of out-door museum. The whole project was envisaged as an educational venture as much as a means of providing the townsmen with fresh air and recreation. His arboretum remains today little changed except that the collections of plants have given way to smooth lawns in the interests of economy.

Loudon was also interested in the design of cemeteries, another feature which the growth of industrial towns called into being to replace the churchyards of former times; and botanical gardens were close to his heart. He was largely responsible for the intro-duction of the term 'gardenesque' to describe the type of gardening where the plants, trees, shrubs and flowers are the most important component of the garden, the design being arranged to display each to its best advantage.

The arboretum and pinetum became the hobby of enthusiasts stimulated by the numerous varieties of trees introduced from newly explored parts of the world. The western regions of the USA were a

38. The Derby Arboretum is the earliest purpose-planned and built public park. It was designed by J. C. Loudon and opened in 1840. The low hillocks were artificial and were intended to vary an otherwise flat uninteresting site.

particularly rich source and collections of as many species as possible would constitute an arboretum. If limited to conifers, and most of the introductions were conifers, the collection would become a pinetum. In many cases the collection was arranged as a sort of garden. Dropmore in Buckinghamshire is an outstanding example of this type of collection.

Paxton

Sir Joseph Paxton (1803-65) was one of the outstanding characters of his time and a man of widely varying interests. Known today chiefly as the designer of the Crystal Palace for the 1851 Exhibition in Hyde Park, he had careers as an architect, a railway director, a member of Parliament and in several other fields. But he began as a gardener, becoming head gardener to the sixth Duke of Devonshire at Chatsworth in 1826. His work there was distinguished particularly by the original design and contruction of a range of glasshouses which were to lead to the design of the Crystal Palace. Within them he cultivated, with great success, the newly arrived tender plants from the far corners of the world. The culmi-

39. This Italianate terrace garden at Harewood House, West Yorkshire, was constructed between 1843 and 1848 by Sir Charles Barry as a foreground to the view from the house of the landscape park laid out by 'Capability' Brown from 1772.

nation was in the flowering in 1849 of the giant water-lily *Victoria amazonica* (*regia*), which was so large that it had to have a glasshouse all to itself.

Paxton the garden designer was, curiously enough, much less forward-looking and inventive than in his other fields of activity. Most of his garden layouts are in the Italianate manner of his time, as in the terraces at Chatsworth and the vast layout at Sydenham around his reconstructed Crystal Palace. In his designs for parks, as opposed to gardens, he tended to follow the precepts of Loudon with his gardenesque ideas. There is little of his work to be seen at Sydenham now but at Chatsworth it is largely intact, and his public parks (Prince's Park, Liverpool; Birkenhead Park; The People's Park, Halifax; and the Cemetery at Coventry) remain to testify to his skill, not as an innovator, but as a practitioner working within the framework of an accepted convention of design.

Public parks

Public parks largely owe their origin to this period, although the Royal Parks of London had been open to the public for some time. They evolved in response to the need for some sort of open space in the growing industrial towns, where people might walk. Soon provision was made for such activities as cricket, archery and putting. The usual design adopted derived mainly from that of the landscape garden as practised by Repton. This was suitable in providing wide grass areas and belts of trees, which were reasonably easy to maintain, and in enabling a large number of people to use the park at one time. The style also provided thick belts of trees around the perimeter of the site to block out what were often unsightly surroundings and thus keep the workaday at bay. Public taste naturally demanded some areas in these parks planted with the showy flowers then in vogue and such areas were laid out on 'gardenesque' lines, usually incorporating areas of formal design with much use of bedding plants. The latter would often depict the coat of arms of the town with the name of the mayor. Such exercises in the carpet bedders' art may still be seen in our public parks in some towns. Clocks set out in bedding plants, with plants even on the hands of the clock, were once a popular feature. The famous one in Princes Street Gardens, Edinburgh, is a rare survivor and as such a valuable historical object.

Robinson and the wild garden

By the 1870s there was again a feeling among a discerning few that the then generally accepted style of garden design had run its course and that the Italianate gardens, stocked with exotic plants from all over the world, were not perhaps the best way to plan

40. *The terraced gardens at Bowood, Wiltshire, provide a formal fore-ground to what remains of the great house. The upper terrace was designed by Sir Robert Smirke in 1818, the lower terrace being added in 1853.*

English gardens in an English climate. One of these few was William Robinson (1839-1935), an Irishman by origin, who decided that it was high time to go back to the plant itself as the source of inspiration in the making of a garden. Even the word 'design' was rejected by him, the plants together making up the garden.

Robinson was insistent also on the value of native plants which could be relied upon to grow well in England. The mere fact that a plant had travelled halfway across the world, or simply that it was difficult to grow, was not to him a sufficient reason for its having a place in the garden. Robinson reserved a special degree of scorn for carpet bedding and topiary, but any practice whereby the hand of man, or design by man, in any way conflicted with the growth and display of the plant as a plant was to him anathema.

Robinson advocated a new type of garden, the wild or natural garden. Here plants were planted out in their natural setting or something approximating to it. They were subtly grouped to display their contrasting forms to best advantage and even Robinson was obliged to admit eventually that this constituted design of a kind. Special kinds of wild garden might be made; beneath trees with woodland plants and in open situations with heathers and low-growing plants. The Robinsonian concept of the wild garden was to have very great influence in the latter years of the nineteenth century and even more in the following century.

Blomfield and the formal garden

Robinson's views, expressed in the most dogmatic manner in his extensive writings, did not pass without challenge. Sir Reginald Blomfield (1856-1942), a distinguished architect, took up the cause of the formal garden in equally dogmatic terms (he seems to have been the first to use the term 'formal garden'). To him gardens were primarily works of art, indeed 'high art' as understood by Ruskin and his disciples. It followed that the hand of man must be everywhere in the garden, with plants doing little more than supply the filling between the various architectural features, balustrades, steps, arcaded walks and pergolas.

Victorian features

Greenhouses and conservatories are particularly characteristic of Victorian England. As we have seen, it took a long time for gardeners to realise that plants need light as well as warmth, but in the mid nineteenth century various methods were evolved of constructing virtually all-glass buildings using cast iron as well as light

41. The Palm House at the Royal Botanic Gardens, Kew, Surrey, built between 1844 and 1848, and designed by the architect Decimus Burton and the engineer Richard Turner.

timber frameworks. Hot water heating was perfected a little earlier and thus the greenhouse was ready to receive the influx of exotic, tender plants which were being introduced from abroad. A conservatory was originally just another word for a greenhouse but in the nineteenth century the term 'conservatory' became restricted to a glass structure attached to the house which could be used as an addition to the living rooms.

Another feature especially associated with the Victorians is the fernery. During the late nineteenth and early twentieth centuries there was a great vogue for the cultivation of ferns, especially the numerous introduced species. Special heated glasshouses were built for them and outdoor ferneries were commonplace. From that time the popularity of ferns declined almost to extinction but it has revived once more in recent years.

Rustic work was also a favourite of the Victorians. The construction of garden furniture and buildings from wood with the bark left on really goes back to the origins of romanticism. The vogue for grottoes is evidence of a similar intellectual attitude to nature. In the nineteenth century garden seats, garden-houses, dairies and even hunting lodges were built in this way, often with thatched roofs to complete the rustic look. Later rustic seats and garden houses were made in cast iron and the former were a favourite with railway companies for station seats.

42. A rustic boat house, from an engraving in 'The Floral World and Garden Guide', 1877.

43. *The garden at Hestercombe House, Somerset, designed by Sir Edwin Lutyens, with planting by Gertrude Jekyll, and constructed from 1904. The rill, seen here, enables water-loving plants to be grown and directs the eye to the open country beyond the garden. Such an oriental feature was, perhaps, strangely prophetic for the later designer of New Delhi.*

5
Modern gardens

As the twentieth century opened there were thus two main styles of gardening in practice: the plantsman's or wild garden as advocated by Robinson, and the formal garden as advocated by Blomfield. Neither of these protagonists could see any common ground, but others saw that the very contrast between the two offered considerable scope if applied to different parts of the same garden. Such a garden might be divided up into a number of areas of unequal size, perhaps those larger in area being devoted to wild or natural gardening, with smaller enclosures, probably close to the house, set out on formal lines with vistas perhaps penetrating into the wild areas to bind the parts of the garden into an integrated whole.

A number of distinguished gardens of this type were developed during the early part of the present century. Perhaps the best known is that of Hidcote Manor in Gloucestershire, now owned by the National Trust, where the observer walks through a series of enclosures, of varying size and scale, formed by high hedges, each with its own strongly marked character. These are contrasted with extensive areas of wild garden. The garden was the work of its owner, Lawrence Johnston, who set out a clear formal framework and then planted it with such a profusion of fine plants as almost to create a naturalistic effect as well. From the small enclosed gardens one passes along great green vistas leading the eye out across the surrounding countryside, then along the valley of a stream planted thickly with water-loving plants, then into yet wilder areas where shrubs grow amid rough grass. There are smooth expanses of lawn edged by noble trees. The outstanding impression is of the pleasures of contrast between gardens of very varied character.

Hidcote can almost be said to have given birth to a style of its own which became the dominant style for the first half of the century. Sissinghurst Castle, Kent, is similar to Hidcote in being the work of devoted owners, Victoria Sackville-West and her husband Sir Harold Nicolson, and now also in the care of the National Trust. While much smaller than Hidcote, there is the same delight in contrast between small enclosed gardens, long vistas and wild areas.

Gertrude Jekyll

An important figure in this phase is Gertrude Jekyll (1843-1932) who grasped the need for design in the arrangement of one plant with another which was inherent in even the Robinsonian approach to the garden. She is particularly associated with the development of the herbaceous border, consisting of hardy plants of good form

44. A view of the early twentieth-century gardens at Hever Castle, Kent, laid out for the American millionaire W. W. Astor. There is an old English garden as well as the Italian garden which is seen here.

45. Hidcote Manor Garden, Gloucestershire, was created by Lawrence Johnston over many years during the early twentieth century. There is a series of contrasting sheltered gardens, such as the one seen here, divided by hedges and topiary features, as well as a stream garden and long allées opening up views over the Cotswold countryside.

in themselves, yet so arranged as to provide an interesting and harmonious whole. Miss Jekyll also evolved principles of colour planning based upon such ideas as that blue flowers and bluish foliage planted at a distance from the observer and red flowers and strong green foliage in the foreground would suggest greater distance and be more sympathetic in appearance. Much of the inspiration for these ideas came from traditional cottage gardens.

Cottage gardens

As succeeding styles came and departed in the gardens of big houses those of humble cottages remained timeless creations quite unaffected by the passing of the years. Of all the styles of garden making considered in these pages that of the cottage garden stands apart from the others, which are ways of making gardens for the well-to-do.

Few of the cottages seen in the countryside today are older than the sixteenth century, when there was a wave of rebuilding in the southern and eastern parts of England. In the north and west this rebuilding came in the seventeenth century. Our cottage gardens

46. Sissinghurst Castle, Kent. This series of interconnecting gardens was created from 1930 by Victoria Sackville-West and Sir Harold Nicolson between the surviving fragments and walls of the castle. The famous White Garden is here seen from the tower, which acts as a focus for the whole layout.

cannot therefore be older than this.

The bounds of the garden are usually clearly defined by a substantial wall, fence or hedge. Stone walls will be used in hill country, brick elsewhere, but in all cases creating a feeling of snugness and cosy enclosure for the countryman who spent his working life in the fields and who liked a contrast from their openness when he came home.

The most important point about the plants grown in the cottage garden is that none of them came from a nurseryman. Many would be given by friends, be struck from cuttings or be handed down from the previous generation. All were planted in the garden wherever there happened to be room. The result was that jumble of multi-coloured plants, giving an impression of a leafy and flowery jungle, which always springs to mind with the words 'cottage garden'. Somehow the colours never seemed to jar and the whole combines with artless simplicity. Usually there would be a few fruit trees, apples mostly, and an evergreen shrub or two grown large from a gift from a friend. Often, too, there would be a coniferous tree standing as a reminder of a Christmas tree of many years ago.

Every good cottage garden had climbers, roses and honeysuckle, jasmine and clematis, climbing up the walls of the cottage and the inevitable wooden sheds, climbing up flimsy trellis work and arching over the cottage door.

Cottage gardens of this traditional kind are getting rarer with every year that passes, as the old cottages give way to the bungalows and semi-detached houses of our own day. But here and there newer houses have gardens which begin to develop along the old lines, so perhaps the cottage garden will survive.

The secret of making a cottage garden is time; time to absorb the feeling of the place, time for each new plant to be assimilated comfortably into its setting; time for the gardener to learn to know his garden and its plants really thoroughly.

Garden design today

Gardens have often, in the past, been influenced by the associated arts of architecture and painting and this is still true today. The influence of modern architecture and modern painting have been considerably delayed in their effect upon gardens but perhaps this delay is of a respectable antiquity, for Sir Francis Bacon (1561-1626) in his essay *On Gardens* wrote that 'Men come to build stately, sooner than to garden finely'. Here and there tentative efforts were made to evolve a new kind of garden, owing little or nothing to past styles and in tune with the life of the twentieth century, but it is only very recently that it has become possible to

47. The swimming pool added to Buscot Park, Oxfordshire, in the 1930s. It is a splendid example of a feature of modern gardens which it is often difficult to integrate into its setting. The pavilion seen beyond the pool contains a squash court and theatre.

describe a style of garden design which is really the counterpart of contemporary architecture.

The clear, geometric forms of modern buildings are reflected in the layout of the formal areas where paving and the outline of pools and planted areas are all of simple design. There is usually an emphatic contrast between the small formal areas and the larger informal ones. This balance is, in large measure, dictated by maintenance considerations in an age where garden labour is both scarce and expensive. The design of the informal areas is usually in a continuation of the garden tradition which resulted from the efforts of William Robinson and Gertrude Jekyll, with the emphasis on the free growth of hardy plants so arranged as to show the plants off to advantage. There is commonly little interest in long formal vistas. The areas near the house tend to be formal with a clean break from where the informal areas extend to the outer parts of the garden.

Perhaps the outstanding fact about garden design today is that entirely new kinds of garden have to be designed — roof gardens for department stores, gardens around and within office buildings and factories (not only for the use of workers during the lunch break but also as a 'prestige' advertisement for the owners), and gardens within housing areas.

The private garden has greatly decreased in area. Even the larg-

48. *The herb garden at Emmanuel College, Cambridge, planted in 1960 to the design of John Codrington. The triangular beds allow paths to cross the court directly to doorways.*

49. *Lea Rhododendron Gardens, Derbyshire, have been developed since 1935 in an old gritstone quarry where the shrubs could be grown beneath the light shade of older silver birch and scots pine trees. Woodland gardens such as this represent a distinctive twentieth-century contribution to the range of garden types previously developed.*

est private garden is but an acre or two in area. To offset this decrease there has been a vast increase in the number of private gardens, all designed and maintained by their owners. Interest in the cultivation and maintenance of gardens has never been higher but a disinterested inspection of a sample of small gardens will soon reveal a depressing lack of ability and even interest in the design of these small rectangular plots. The design problem they pose is admittedly one which would have taxed the abilities of Le Notre and Capability Brown combined, but it must be hoped that a great improvement will result from the increasing public interest in the quality of the environment in which we all have to live. The garden is but an environment, and the one over which we have the greatest degree of control.

50. A garden in a contemporary manner designed by Dame Sylvia Crowe at a research station near Slough, Berkshire. Such modern gardens, deriving their inspiration from modern architecture, are still rare in Britain.

6
Oriental gardens

At various periods oriental gardens have influenced the design of English gardens. Chinese and Japanese gardens have been those principally concerned but Indian gardens inspired at least the solitary example of Sezincote in Gloucestershire, where Humphry Repton created an Anglo-Indian water garden to compliment the extraordinary house. Arab gardens have had a little influence too, almost entirely by way of Spanish gardens, but minimal in extent when compared with those of China and Japan.

Chinese gardens first began to interest gardeners in western Europe towards the end of the seventeenth century. The Chinese garden is based upon the veneration of nature as seen in the mountains, rocks, valleys, lakes and waterfalls of the Chinese landscape. The garden is a representation of this landscape but carried out with an economy of means which is only paralleled in Chinese landscape painting where the long scroll will represent the landscape with just a suggestion of the main features. The rest is left to the imagination, for the art of the Chinese is more in the mind than in the artefact.

The garden thus becomes just a suggestion of an idealised landscape leaving the mind of the observer to complete the picture. A Chinese garden is a place in which to stroll slowly, to pause frequently and to think deeply. Paths wander and wind, there are steep bridges to encourage one to pause and contemplate the view over the water. The garden is withdrawn from the outside world, a refuge from the wider landscape but at the same time a re-creation of it in idealised form.

Japan derived this tradition of the garden from China but it developed gardens which tend to be firmer in design and more clearly expressed. There are well recognised forms of Japanese gardens. The flat garden may be simply an expanse of sand carefully raked to a pattern and embellished with a composition of rock, an ornament, such as a lantern, and a plant. The dry garden is similar but has mounds to simulate hills. Water is suggested only by rocks suitably placed. The hill and water garden has sinuous watercourses with islands which are arranged around groups of mounds. The degree of elaboration varies but always certain rules are observed. Plants are used to complement the picture and are often an essential feature but they must conform in placing, size and shape. Those most favoured are rounded and even gnarled in appearance. Dwarf conifers are obviously suited to this type of garden, as are azaleas which can be contrasted with the verticality of bamboos.

Clearly, gardens of this kind have certain affinities with English landscape gardens of the eighteenth century, and an interest in Chinese gardens was undoubtedly a factor in the new thinking about gardens which was taking place in the early part of that century. But many other factors contributed to the new thinking and it would be an exaggeration to describe the landscape gardens of the eighteenth century as any kind of Chinese garden. Yet there is the same attempt to create an idealised version of the natural landscape and the same emphasis on the form of natural things and on balance as opposed to symmetry. The difference arises from the nature of the English landscape garden as an idealisation and, indeed, exploitation of the landscape of the particular place where the garden is made, whilst the Chinese or Japanese garden is a re-creation of a conception of the ideal in landscape related to no particular place and certainly not to that of the place where the garden is situated.

There have been a number of Japanese gardens created in Britain during the present century, with varying degrees of authenticity. From a purely constructional and horticultural point of view few garden styles could be easier to work within but a thorough understanding of the original gardens and the philosophy of which they form an expression is essential if anything more than a lifeless copy of the superficialities of the style is not to result. There are few styles of garden design which hold more pitfalls for the unwary.

51. At Shugborough, Staffordshire, is the Chinese House overlooking the river crossed by a cast iron bridge of 1813.

52. *A complex building is set off to best advantage by a simple garden.*

53. *A more elaborate garden suits a simple building.*

7
Gardening in period

It is often said that the great age of gardening is gone for ever and, as we have seen, the making of gardens of more than a few acres is rare today. The exceptions are public spaces and parks and gardens around offices, factories, and public institutions. Yet there has never before been so much gardening and garden-making done as there is today. These new gardens are those of a fraction of an acre which are looked after by their proud owners and are as much a part of their daily lives as the gardens of past centuries were of their owners. Being so small they become almost an outdoor extension of the rooms within the house and at the same time provide the setting for the house as seen by the outside world.

Which style?

Reference has been made to the interdependence of architecture and garden design, and where an old building needs a garden around it one must first decide if any style of garden design from the past should be adopted. The design of the new garden should follow logically from the site and the requirements of those who will use it. The design adopted should compliment the building for which it provides the setting. In general, complicated building with much small detail will look best set in a garden with broad, uncluttered spaces; the reverse also applies. The problem can be hardest in the case of Victorian houses, often of complex, small-scale design. A garden in a style contemporary with that of the building would result in an elaborate and detailed layout which might fail to set off the building to advantage. A more satisfactory solution might include just a few features characteristic of Victorian gardens: a small area of bedding plants in a rectangular, formal area with the remainder of the garden a simple expanse of lawn, with trees and shrubs selected from those commonly grown during the period, around the boundaries of the garden. The result would not be a Victorian garden as such but it would present just a flavour of that period in an otherwise modern garden.

Although in the case of earlier periods the problem is easier, the answer does not simply depend upon the date of the building, for there was usually a considerable time lag between architecture and garden design and it is generally best to look forward from the date of the building for up to thirty years to find a design sympathetic to the character of the house.

How far to go

The urge to pursue historical accuracy must not be pushed too far. A garden of a past age, correct in all details, might be interesting to students of the history of garden design but it has to be lived with in the twentieth century. Few people today would like to live with a Tudor garden with its profusion of small wooden statues and rails painted in bright colours. Some features of Tudor gardens may be attractive today but not all.

There are a number of practical difficulties in the way of a thorough historical garden reconstruction. The main one is the difficulty and cost of the maintenance of the finished garden. In past centuries gardeners were plentiful and poorly paid. Today this is not so but the need to give adequate maintenance to the completed garden is of the first importance and so often the enthusiasm for creating a garden is greater than enthusiasm for its subsequent maintenance. A possible exception to this may be the landscape gardens of the eighteenth century but this is a style little applicable to present day conditions, since a large area is essential to obtain an authentic effect.

Victorian carpet bedding demands the most labour, whereas a wild garden as advocated by William Robinson is obviously better adapted to present-day conditions. Indeed, the success which Robinson enjoyed in vanquishing the carpet bedders was partly because of the expensive maintenance at a time when incomes were falling.

Unless the garden is being made purely as a historical reconstruction, it will have to serve certain modern uses, such as providing outdoor living space. Moreover, there often seems to be something particularly lifeless about historical reconstructions, though as gardens contain living plants there are limits to the extent to which they can be kept to a rigid plan.

This is not to argue that gardens designed in a past style have no place in modern garden making. Given a modern building, there is an overwhelming case for surrounding it with a garden which will be an expression of the needs and aspirations of our own times, but where a building of a past age requires a sympathetic setting, and other practical requirements can be met, there is much to be said for making a garden which represents something of a pastiche of our own time with that of the time when the building was designed.

Gardens made as accurately as possible in past styles do have great value as educational and horticultural examples. Several such reconstructions have been made in recent years, mainly attached to museums, and are noted in chapter 9. Whilst all have been modified to some degree to suit their present purpose as museum exhibits, they convey very vividly just what it was like to walk about in a garden several centuries ago.

Planting in period

Most plants grown today, and available through the nursery trade, are the result of a long series of improvements in breeding. In some cases it is possible to obtain plants of fairly similar form to those grown in the past. A sensible alternative is to grow plants which will make an effect similar to those of the past. If one grows the descendants of earlier plants the visual effects will differ considerably from those of a garden of the past age.

When selecting plants for period gardens one may decide to choose those introduced to this country during the period in question, but normally some years elapsed between the introduction of a plant and its widespread cultivation. As such gardens are at least intended to be evocative of the period it is well to emphasise plants which are particularly characteristic of the time. Thus towards the end of the seventeenth century the interest in growing tulips developed into a mania. Wealthy men nearly beggared themselves to obtain a rare bulb and so tulips are especially associated with this phase of strong Dutch influence on English gardens.

At the same time some plants, much grown in one period, continued in favour almost indefinitely. This is most true of the rose, which has never lost the affections of English gardeners. Even so, our modern roses are such that no Victorian would recognise, so greatly has the appearance of these plants been developed. The old type of roses have recently staged something of a revival, with the result that 'old fashioned' roses are now easily obtainable from nurseries. Lists of plants suitable for period gardens are given at the back of this book.

8
The restoration of gardens

Gardens are places where the hand of man is uppermost over nature. Once that hand is removed nature soon takes over control and the garden deteriorates and may soon be lost for ever. Garden design can thus be one of the most ephemeral of the arts and gardens of past ages are difficult to preserve. They are largely composed of plants which have an allotted life span and need replacement. So great is this problem that few gardens of former times have come down to us in anything like their original form. Often all traces have gone and an attractive old building is bereft of its setting.

How much restoration?

The nature of a restoration scheme depends greatly upon the extent of our knowledge of the previous layout. There may be surviving features still visible and more may be found by archaeological excavation. Written records, plans and surveys may survive which can be invaluable. In some cases it is thus possible to restore the design with almost complete certainty. At Kirby Hall in Northamptonshire archaeologists have discovered remains of the Great Garden of 1685-6 just below the present-day ground surface and restoration can therefore proceed with an unusual degree of assurance.

There may be old drawings and engravings of the early garden, or even photographs of Victorian gardens, but even where they exist they are all too often of very limited use in recovering the original layout. Inevitably a good deal of imagination will have to be used in planning the restoration and the result may well be satisfactory only as a garden of a previous age translated into twentieth century terms.

Much the most common situation is for just a few trees and perhaps barely discernible traces of terracing to remain from the old garden. A few well grown trees can add immeasurably to the appearance of any garden and one can use these remains as the basis for a garden which, whilst providing a suitable setting for the building, otherwise owes nothing to the garden design of the period when the building was erected.

If it is decided to try to recreate the old garden it is necessary to appreciate at the outset that this will really be a new garden even though it may incorporate features from the old layout. A free adaptation of the design features of the past period is perhaps a better aim than a painstaking reproduction. One should beware of incorporating wholesale features from other places which may well not look satisfactory on another site. An exception to this might perhaps be made in the case of such self-contained details as the design of parterres and knot gardens. At Pitmedden in Grampian the National Trust for Scotland have very successfully recreated the seventeenth-century Great Garden with parterres to a design derived from a seventeenth-century view of the gardens of Holyroodhouse Palace, Edinburgh. In this case there was reason to suppose that the design of the two gardens would have been similar, but elsewhere, whilst the details can perhaps be derived from such sources, the overall layout must be related to the site and its intended use.

In some restoration schemes the designer is almost embarrassed by having too much information about the previous state of the garden. Where a garden has existed for several centuries the layout may have passed through a series of changes. Many an owner has been content, or obliged by lack of money, to live in a house of former times built in a style long out of fashion. Very rarely have owners been content to leave their garden in the state in which it was bequeathed to them. The cost of alterations to a garden is much less than that of alterations to a house and the evolutionary nature of a garden, composed of living plants, means that the garden has to be renewed, with the inevitable changes in planting.

The restorer must then decide which of the former states of the garden is to become the basis of the restoration scheme. In practice the answer will usually depend upon considerations of practicability of maintenance and by a desire to incorporate the most attractive and interesting features into the restored garden which will give most pleasure and satisfaction to present day users. The result may well be an amalgam of gardens of various periods.

Gardens in evolution

Gardens are composed of living things which, after their allotted span of growth and development, wither and are no more. This simple fact has important consequences for the gardener in dealing with old gardens.

The original plants in the garden get larger with the years and while this is of little consequence in the case of short-lived plants, when one considers long-lived plants, the result may well be quite different to that intended by the original designer. Thus yew hedges form the structural framework of many fine gardens. When first planted they probably had little effect in creating the desired sense of enclosure, but within a few years the hedges would be serving their purpose well enough. Clipping, if carried out regularly, will tend to keep the shrubs to the desired size but, inevitably, as the years pass into centuries, the hedge will get bigger, not only in width but also in height, and much the same process takes place with shrubs treated as topiary. The justly famous topiary garden at Levens Hall in Cumbria now has enormous examples of the topiarist's art which quite overwhelm the garden, but this must be far from the intention of Beaumont when he laid it out in 1689.

There are two ways to approach such problems. One can clear the overgrown plants and start again with new ones, leaving one's descendants to decide when the new plants grow too large, or one can accept the larger plants as part of the evolving pattern of the garden and adjust the design to accommodate them in proportion. Such adjustments might well involve enlarging the main compartments of the garden by removing dividing hedges or increasing the apparent extent of part of the garden by replacing shrub planting with clear lawns.

When trees grow beyond their intended bounds the result may be a dank, airless and overshadowed area of the garden. The remedy may involve thinning the trees drastically because the original designer may have planted his trees thickly for reasonably quick effects and assumed that those who followed would carry out thinning. Very often those in charge many years later fail to do so, either from neglect or from misplaced respect for the work of the past.

There are, however, other factors at work in changing the appearance of gardens as the years go by. Rapidly rising costs of maintenance have meant that owners have frequently had to reduce costs by simplifying many features. Parterres and knot gardens and Victorian carpet bedding features have suffered especially severely in this way, often being replaced by lawns. The result may be satisfactory as a twentieth-century garden, especially if surrounding trees and shrubs have grown to great size, but it will not be the garden intended by the original designer.

Trees have a longer life span than any other plants in a garden but as they grow old they change in form, losing that regularity of shape which is so attractive a feature of a tree in its prime. The structure of the tree loosens up and a less regular form is the result. Formal gardens of the seventeenth century depend for no small part of their effect upon the cliff-like edges of the plantations of trees which commonly surround these gardens. Once this regularity is lost the garden takes on an altogether more romantic appearance.

The time comes when trees die or become diseased and have to be felled. The wise gardener will have foreseen this and will have younger trees coming along to take over the function of the old ones. All too often there has been no such provision and a heart-rending decision has to be made which will affect the appearance of the garden for at least the next twenty years. Modern techniques of moving semi-mature trees, descended from methods used as far back as the eighteenth century, can be of great assistance if the

54. *The rustic cottage forms the centrepiece of the Swiss Garden at Old Warden, Bedfordshire. In the 1820s Lord Ongley entertained his friends here amidst a carefully contrived, small-scale jardin orné.*

number of trees involved is reasonably small, or just enough to help the garden over that period of desolation which the sudden removal of large trees can bring, and whilst newly planted trees are growing up to take over.

Trees can be a minor problem in some types of garden. In others they are vital. The outstanding cases are eighteenth-century landscape gardens which rely for their effects upon rolling turf and fine trees. Today we see all these landscape gardens and parks in decline as the trees pass maturity and slowly disintegrate. What can be done? Clearly, replanting is essential but unless one is prepared to fell all the trees they cannot be replanted on the same spot. Overshadowing of the old trees usually precludes this and where old trees have been felled removal of the stumps to allow new trees to be planted can be expensive. Clear felling should always be avoided if at all possible, for then the entire effect is gone. Sometimes new trees can be planted in gaps in plantations where old trees have fallen. Entire clumps and groups of trees can be planted, possibly in places not intended by the original designer but reflecting his original intentions and also contributing something new to the landscape.

Avenues of trees pose particularly difficult problems when they pass maturity. As the trees decay should they be replaced one by one, with the inevitable gap-toothed effect? Should the entire avenue be felled and a new one planted? Avenues rely for their effect upon their regularity. The whole is greater than the sum of the parts and each tree loses its identity in the long corridor of foliage. Replacing each tree as and when it decays can rarely be satisfactory, especially in the case of single avenues. Where there are double, or even treble, rows of trees, as in the case of the great lime avenue in Clumber Park, Nottinghamshire, the objections to this method are much reduced because the gaps are covered by the trees in the adjoining rows.

Clear felling and replanting is often the only practicable policy but it is one which requires courage and a degree of self-denial for a significant segment of a human lifetime. The well known Long Walk in Windsor Great Park had to be subjected to such treatment in 1945 when the limes planted by order of Charles II had rotted beyond redemption. Today one may admire the replacement avenue but for many years the landscape setting of the approach to the castle was much impaired. One way of avoiding an interval of a quarter century or so is to plant another avenue a little outside or inside the lines of the decaying one. The young trees may suffer somewhat from overshadowing but they should make some headway to prepare for the time when the old trees are felled and they succeed to their roles. The new avenue will not be the same width as the old but the variation will be a small price to pay for a smooth transition.

Time can also be unkind to water features. In the case of small pools, cascades and fountains the problems of restoration are reasonably straightforward, involving cleaning and replacing defective equipment. Where large sheets of water are concerned the problems are more difficult. Many landscape gardens depend for their effect upon a lake occupying the lowest part of the ground and seeming to be an inevitable and supremely natural feature of the landscape. Usually this lake is quite artificial, probably a stream of insignificant dimensions which the designer has dammed up to provide the noble stretch of water. The lake may well be quite shallow over the greater part of its area. As the years go by purely natural processes, decay of water plants, silting from the faster flowing water of the stream being checked by the stationary waters of the lake, will lead to the lake becoming progressively shallower. Eventually water plants will appear on the surface and later still marsh conditions will develop. The visual effect of such conditions can be disastrous. The delights of the water with its dappled surface reflecting the sky and its clear outline emphasising the contours of the surrounding land is replaced by an untidy mass of vegetation which entirely lacks that contrast which is one of the principal pleasures of a lake set in parkland. The first reaction of a hard-pressed owner may well be to accept these results as inevitable and hope for the best. This will hardly ever be satisfactory. The replacement of a lake by any form of vegetation will usually upset the appearance of the landscape garden, comparable in effect only to the felling of all the trees. Restoration of the clear waters of the lake should be regarded as a first priority in the work of restoration. Cleaning and dredging to increase the depth of water will be of great assistance and future trouble can be avoided by increasing the speed of flow of water through the lake. Creating conditions of biological balance in the plant and animal life in the lake is also important so that particularly rampant species do not achieve dominance. Even so, one should accept that every century or so major cleaning will be required as the price one has to pay for the pleasures of looking at a landscape embellished by a lake.

Nature as master?

All the garden makers whose work has been reviewed in these pages endeavoured to create a garden which would be an idealised expression of nature. This is quite obviously so in the case of the eighteenth-century landscape garden but it is so also in the case of gardens of other periods. The variations arise from inherent differences in man's ideals of nature. Renaissance man saw nature as a system of pre-ordained elements which encompassed the whole of life. His garden, therefore, gave expression, in its formal layout, to this strongly hierarchical view of nature.

Today this view of nature is remote from our own. Yet in order to be able to recreate a garden in the manner of those made in response to this very different stimulus we must try to understand the motivations of those who evolved that type of garden. Even in the case of a period as recent as the mid nineteenth century, with its optimistic view of the inevitability of human progress, we experience great difficulty in coming to terms with the thought behind the gardens of the time.

In the case of styles of gardening developed by cultures differing widely in space as well as in time the problems are greater still. The traditional gardens of the Orient pose difficulties in the appreciation of the philosophical approach of the original designers which must be ovecome if more than a reproduction of the superficialities of the style is to result.

Gardens are the creations of an age at most, not of eternity. Just to enjoy gardens of whatever style is sufficient justification for their making.

9
Plants for period gardens

The lists of plants which follow have been prepared as a guide as to which plants are appropriate to each of the five main periods of garden making. For each period, flowers and trees and shrubs are listed separately. Terminal dates for the periods have been determined rather loosely and some plants known to have been introduced to Britain in one period are listed in the following one as not being in general garden cultivation until the later period. Some native plants are included in the period during which they began to be cultivated in gardens.

Strictly defined, the lists are of plants grown in gardens at the end of the period in question. It can, of course, be generally assumed that the plants listed under all the preceding periods would be available.

The lists owe much to two books by Alice M. Coats: *Flowers and Their Histories* (A. & C. Black, second edition 1968), and *Garden Shrubs and Their Histories* (Vista Books, 1963), and the period gardener is directed to these for further details.

MEDIEVAL
FLOWERS

Achillea millefolium
Allium ursinum
Althea rosea
Anemone coronaria
  A. hepatica
Antirrhinum majus
Aquilegia vulgaris
Bellis perennis (single)
Campanula repunculus
  C. rotundifolia
  C. glomerata
Centranthus ruber
Chieranthus cheiri
Chrysanthemum leucanthemum
  C. parthenium
Crocus aureus
  C. vernus
  C. luteus
  C. sativus
Dianthus caryophyllus

D. plumarius
D. barbatus
D. carthusianorum
Doronicum pardalianches
  D. plantagineum
Epilobium angustifolium
Euphorbia cyparissias
Galanthus nivalis
Geranium pratense
  G. phaeum
  G. sanguineum
Helleborus niger
Iris pseudacorus
  I. germanica
Lilium candidum
Linum usitatissimum
  L. perenne
Lychnis chalcedonica (single)
Matthiola incana
Nepeta cataria

Paeonia masculata
Papaver somniferum
Physalis alkekengi
Primula acaulis
Verbascum thapsis

Verbena officinalis
Vinca minor
  V. major
Viola odorata

TREES AND SHRUBS

Acer pseudoplatanus
Buxus sempervirens
Cistus
Cytisus scoparius
Euonymus
Genista anglica
  G. pilosa
Hippophae rhamnoides
Hypericum perforatum
  H. androseanum
Laburnum vulgare

Laurus nobilis
Ligustrum vulgare
Lonicera periclymenum
Rosa gallica
  R. g. officinalis
  R. alba
  R. rubiginosa
Ulex europaeus
  U. minor
  U. gallii

TUDOR
FLOWERS

Acanthus mollis
Achillea ptarmica
Aconitum napellus
  A. anthora
  A. variegatum
  A. lycoctonum
Althea cannabina
Alyssum maritimum
Amaranthus cordatus
  A. hypochondriacus
Anchusa italica
  A. officinalis
  A. sempervirens
  A. tinctoria
Anemone nemorosa
  A. apennina
  A. pulsatilla
Anthemis pyrethrum
Anthericum liliago
Armeria maritima

Asphodeline lutea
Asphodelus albus
  A. fistulosus
  A. ramosus
Aster amellus
  A. tripolium
Astrantia major
Bellis perennis (double)
Callendula officinalis
Campanula medium
  C. trachelium
  C. persicifolia
Canna indica
Cardamine pratensis
Catananche coerulea
Centaurea cyanus
  C. montana
Chrysanthemum segetum
Colchicum autumnale
Convallaria majalis

Corydalis bulbosa
  C. cava
  C. claviculata
  C. lutea
Cyclamen hederaefolium
  C. europaeum
Delphinium staphisagria
  D. consolida
  D. ajacis
Dictamnus fraxinella
Digitalis purpurea
Eranthus hyemalis
Eryngium maritimum
  E. planum
  E. campestre
  E. alpinum
Erythronium dens-canis
Filipendula ulmaria
  F. hexapetala
Fritillaria imperialis
  F. meleagris
Galega officinalis
Gentiana lutea
  G. cruciata
  G. acaulis
  G. campestris
  G. pneumonanthe
Geranium tuberosum
Gladiolus illyricus
  G. communis
  G. segetum
  G. imbricatum
Helianthus annuus
  H. multiflorus
Hemerocallis fulva
  H. flava
Hesperis matronalis
Hibiscus trionum
Hyacinthus orientalis
Iberis umbellata
Iris sibirica
  I. susiana
  I. tuberosa
  I. xiphioides
  I. xiphium

Lactuca perennis
  L. alpina
Lathyrus latifolia
Lavendula spica
Leucojum vernum
  L. aestivum
  L. autumnale
Lilium chalcedonicum
  L. aurantiacum
  L. martagon
Linaria vulgaris
Lunaria biennis
  L. rediviva
Lupinus albus
  L. luteus
  L. varius
Lychnis chalcedonica (double)
  L. coronaria
Lysimachia nummularia
  L. vulgaris
Matthiola annua
Melandrium albus
  M. rubrum
Mirabilis jalapa
Muscari moschatum
  M. comosum
  M. botryoides
  M. neglectum
Narcissus pseudo-narcissus
  N. hispanicus
  N. bicolor
  N. poeticus
  N. tazetta
  N. incomparabilis
  N. biflorus
  N. jonquilla
Nigella sativa
  N. damascena
Ornithogalum umbellatum
Paeonia officinalis
Polemonium coeruleum
Polygonatum multiflorum
Primula veris
  P. auricula
  P. x *pubescens*

Pulmonaria officinalis
Ranunculus aconitifolius
   R. acris fl. pl.
   R. repens
   R. asiaticus
Salvia horminum
   S. sclarea
   S. turkestanica
   S. pratensis
Saponaria officinalis fl. pl.
   S. vaccaria
Scilla bifolia
   S. amoena
   S. lilio-hyacinthus
   S. autumnalis
Sedum acre
   S. anglicanum
   S. reflexum

S. telephinium
Solidago virgaurea
Tagetes erecta
   T. patula
Thalictrum minus
   adiantifolium
Trollius europeus
Tropaeolum minus
Tulipa sylvestris
   T. gesneriana
Veratrum album
   V. nigrum
Verbascum phoeniceum
   V. lychnitis
   V. nigrum
Veronica spicata
   V. teucrium
Viola tricolor

TREES AND SHRUBS

Agave americana
Arbutus unedo
Artemesia abrotanum
Berberis vulgaris
Buxus suffruticosa
Cercis siliquastrum
Cistus albidus
   C. salvifolius
   C. ladaniferus
Clematis vitalba
   C. viticella
   C. flammula
   C. cirrhosa
   C. integrifolia
Colutea arbosescens
Daphne merzereum
   D. laureola
Eleagnus angustifolia
Genista sagittalis
Jasminum officinale
   J. fruticans
Lonicera caprifolium
   L. alpigena

L. xylestreum
Morus nigra
Myrtus communis
Nerium odorum
Paliurus spina-christi
Philadelphus coronarius
Phillyrea angustifolia
   P. latifolia
Phlomis fruticosa
Prunus fruticosa
   P. amygdalus
   P. armeniaca
   P. persica
Punica granata
Quercus ilex
Rhododendron ferrugineum
   R. hirsutum
Robinia pseudacacia
Rosa damascena
   R moschata
   R. centifolia
   R. cinnamomea
   R. x Frankfurt Rose

R. hemispherica
R. foetida
R. f. bicolor
R. villosa
Ruscus hyoglossum
Sambucus nigra
S. n. 'Alba'
S. n. laciniata
S. racemosa

Spartium junceum
Staphylea pinnata
Syringa vulgaris
Tamarix myriceria germanica
T. gallica
Viburnum tinus
Vitex agnus-castus
Yucca gloriosa

STUART
FLOWERS

Alchemilla vulgaris
A. alpina
Allium moly
Alyssum saxatilis
Amaranthus tricolor
Anemone hortensis
A. pavonia
A. stellata
A. ranunculoides
Anthericum ramosum
Aquilegia canadensis
Armeria latifolia
Aruncus sylvester
Aster tradescantia
A. novi-belgiae
Astrantia minor
Caltha palustris fl. pl.
Campanula specularium
Centaurea moschata
C. suaveolens
Chrysanthemum coronarium
C. frutescens
Convolvulus major
C. tricolor
Coreopsis auriculata
Delphinium elatum
Digitalis lutea
D. ferruginea
D. canariensis
Echinacea purpurea

Eryngium amethystinum
Erythronium americanum
Euphorbia lathyrus
Gentiana asclepiadea
Geranium striatum
G. macrorrhizum
Gladiolus imbricatum
G. byzantinus
Gynadriris sisyrinchium
Hedysarum coronarium
Helianthus tuberosus
Helichrysum orientale
Hibiscus syriacus
Hieraceum aurantiacum
Hyacinthus amethystinus
Iberis semperflorens
Impatiens balsamina
I. noli-me-tangere
Iris foetidissima
I. pallida
I. sibirica flexuosa
Kniphofia uvaria
K. pumila
Kochia scoparia trichophylla
Lathyrus odoratus
L. vernus
Lilium maculatum
L. pyrenaicum
L. pomponium
L. canadense

Linaria cymbalaria
  L. purpurea
Lobelia cardinalis
  L. syphilitica
Lupinus hirsutus
  L. perenne
Meconopsis cambrica
Monarda fistulosa
Muscari comosum monstrosum
  M. racemosum
Narcissus alpestris
  N. moschatus
  N. telemanicus plenus
  N. odorus
  N. eystettensis
Nerine sarniensis
Nigella hispanica
Oenothera biennis
Omphalodes linifolia
  O. verna
Ornithogalum arabicum
  O. lutea
  O. pyrenaicum
  O. nutans
Paeonia arietina

P. peregrina
Paradisea liliastrum
Pelargonium pellatum
  P. zonale
  P. triste
Primula acaulis rubra
  P. x *variabilis*
Pulmonaria saccharata
Ranunculus ficaria
Rudbeckia laciniata
Salvia haematadoes
Sanguinaria canadense
Saxifraga umbrosa
  S. granulata
Scabiosa atropurpurea
Scilla peruviana
Senecio elegans
Solidago canadense
Thalictrum glaucum
  T. aquilegifolium
Tradescantia virginiana
Tropaeolum majus
Tulipa suaveolens
  T. clusiana
Verbascum blattaria

TREES AND SHRUBS

Aesculus hippocastanum
  A. pavia
Amelanchier oblongifolia
Campsis radicans
Cedrus libani
Cistus menspeliensis
  C. crispus
  C. populifolius
  C. x *corbariensis*
Colutea orientalis
Cornus stolonifera
Cotoneaster integerrimus
Erica mediterranea
  E. arborea
Euonymus latifolius
  E. americanus

Genista monospermum
Halimium halimifolium
Hedera helix
  H. chrysocarpa
  H. hibernica
Hibiscus syriacus
Hypericum calycinum
Jasminum humile
Larix decidua
Liquidambar styraciflua
Liriodendron tulipifera
Lonicera periclymenum belgica
  L. sempervirens
  L. coerulea
  L. nigra

Lycium chinense
  L. halimifolium
Magnolia virginiana
Parthenocissus quinquefolia
Passiflora incarnata
  P. coerulea
Prunus tenella
  P. lauro-cerasus
Pyracantha coccinea
Rhamnus alertanus
Quercus coccinea
Rhus cotinus
  R. typhina
  R. toxicondendron
  R. radicans
  R. vernix
Rosa gallica versicolor
  R. virginiana

Rubus falcatus
  R. ulmifolius
    bellidiflorus
  R. laciniatus
Ruscus aculeatus
  R. hypophyllum
Spiraea salicifolia
  S. hypericifolia
Syringa persica
  S. p. laciniata
Vitex unedo
Vitis vimifera purpurea
  V. v. apiifolia
  V. aestivalis
  V. lalrusca
  V. vulpina
Yucca filamentosa
  Y. aloifolia

GEORGIAN
FLOWERS

Achillea eupatorium
Alchemilla alpina conjuncta
Alstroemeria pelegrina
Anchusa azurea
Aster grandiflorus
  A. novi-angliae
  A. laevis
Bergenia crassifolia
  B. cordifolia
Bocconia cordata
Brunnera macrophylla
Callistephus chinensis
Camellia coelestris
Campanula carpatica
  C. lactiflora
Catananche bicolor
Cephalaria tartarica
  C. alpina
Chrysanthemum carinetum
  C. maximum
  C. sinensis x indicum
Clarkia pulchella
  C. elegans

Convolvulus scammonia
Coreopsis lanceolata
  C. verticillata
  C. tinctoria
Dahlia pinnata
Delphinium grandiflorum
Dianthus sinensis
Dicentra eximia
Digitalis parviflora
Dimorphotheca pluvialis
  D. aurantiaca
Dodecatheon media
Doronicum caucasicum
Echinacea angustifolia
Erigeron speciosus
  bellidifolius
Eryngium giganteum
Escholtzia californica
Euphorbia marginata
Gaillardia pulchella
  G. aristarta
Galanthus plicatus
Gentiana septemfida

Geum chiloense
Gillenia trifoliata
Gladiolus tristis
Helichrysum arenarium
   H. bracteatum
Heliotropium peruvianum
Hemerocallis minor
Hosta ventricosa
Iberis sempervirens
Ixia maculata
   I. monadelpha
   I. patens
   I. viridiflora
Lathyrus megellanicus
Lepachys pinnata
   L. columnaris
Lilium canadense
   L. philadelphicum
   L. superbum
   L. tigrinum
Linaria dalmatica
Linum narbonense ·
   L. arboreum
   L. flavum
   L. grandiflorum rubra
Lobelia fulgens
   L. erinus
Lupinus arboreus
   L. nootkatensis
   L. polyphyllus
Malcomia maritima
Mesambryanthemum
   crystalinum
Mimulus luteus
   M. moschatus
Monarda didyma
Myosotis palustris
   M. sylvatica
   M. dissitiflora
Narcissus recurvens
Nepeta faassenii
Nymphaea odorata
Oenothera odorata
   O. tetragona var. *fraseri*
   O. missouriensis

   O. amoena
Paeonia lactiflora
   P. whitleyi major
Papaver nudicaule
   P. orientale
   P. bracteatum
   P. rhoeas
Pelargonium hederinum
   P. inquinans
Pentstemon barbatus
Petasites fragrans
Phlox paniculata
Platycodon grandiflorum
Polemonium reptans
   P. humile
Potentilla argyrophylla
   P. atrosanguinea
   P. nepalensis
Pulmonaria angustifolia
Pyrethrum roseum
Ranunculus sanguineus
Reseda odorata
Rudbeckia hirta
Salpiglossis sinuata
Salvia virgata
   S. coccinea
   S. fulgens
   S. splendens
Saxifraga sarmentosa
   S. cordifolia
Scabiosa caucasia
Scilla sibirica
Tagetes minuta
   T. corymba
Tigridia pavonia
Trollius asiaticus
Tropaeolium peregrinum
   T. tuberosum
Tulipa persica
   T. oculis-solis
Veratrum viride
Verbena bonariensis
   V. chamaedrifolia
   V. incisa
   V. tweedii

Veronica longifolia
  V. incana
  V. gentianoides
Viola lutea sudetica
  V. altaica

V. cornuta
Zinnia pauciflora
  Z. elegans
  Z. e. violacea
  Z. e. coccinea

TREES AND SHRUBS

Aesculus octandra
  A. parviflora
Aloysia triphylla
Amelanchier ovalis
  A. confusa
Aristolochia macrophylla
Aucuba japonica
Aurucaria araucana
Azalea ponticum
  Ghent azaleas
Berberis ilicifolia
Buddleia globosa
  B. salvifolia
Calluna sps.
Calycanthus floridus
Camellia chandleri elegans
  C. japonica
  C. reticulata
Campsis chinensis
Ceanothus americanus
Chaenomeles speciosa
Chimonanthus praecox
Choisya ternata
Cistus laurifolius
  C. cyprius
Clematis alpina
  C. florida
  C. orientalis
Colutea istria
Cornus sanguinea
  C. mas
  C. alba
  C. florida
Cotoneaster frigidus
  C. microphyllus
  C. rotundifolius

Cytisus monspessulensis
  C. hirsutus
  C. purgans
  C. austriacus
  C. canariensis
  C. albus
  C. nigricans
  C. purpureus
Daboecia cantabrica
Danae racemosa
Daphne pontica
  D. odora
  D. cneorum
Deutzia scabra
Diervilla lonicera
Drimys winteri
  D. aromatica
Eleagnus argentia
Enkianthus quinqueflorus
Erica cinerea
  E. tetralix
  E. ciliaris
  E. vagans
  E. carnea
  E. lusitanica
  E. australis
  E. terminalis
Euonymus japonicus
  E. atropurpureus
Fuchsia coccinea
  F. megellanica
  F. m. conica
Gaultheria procumbens
  G. 'Shallon'
Genista aetnensis
  G. virgata

Halesia carolina
Halimium umbellatum
  H. lasianthum formosum
  H. ocymoides
Hamamelis virginiana
Helianthemum nummularium
  H. glaucum
  H. alpestre
Hydrangea arborescens
  H. querciflora
  H. hortensia
Jasminum humile 'Revolution'
  J. h. wallichianum
Kalma latifolia
  K. angustifolia
Kerria japonica (double)
Leycesteria formosa
Ligustrum vulgare
  sempervirens
  L. ovalifolium
  L. o. aureum
  L. lucidum
Lonicera periclymenum
  serotina
  L. x italica
  L. japonica
  L. tartarica
Magnolia grandiflora
  M. denudata
  M. lilifolia
  M. soulangeana
Mahonia aquifolia
Nandina domestica
Osmanthus fragrans
Paeonia suffruticosa
Pernettya mucronata
Philadelphus inodorus
  P. pubescens
  P. grandiflorus
Phyllostachys niger
Pieris floribunda
Populus nigra italica
Potentilla fruticosa
  P. davurica
Prunus pumila

P. japonica
P. lucitanica
Pseudotsuga douglasii
Quercus cerris
  Q. lucombeana
Rhododendron maximum
  R. ponticum
  R. caucasium
  R. catawbiense
  R. arboreum
  R. a. x altaclarense
  R. viscosum
  R. nudiflorum
  R. speciosum
  R. calendulaceum
  R. molle
Rhus glabra
Ribes sanguineum
  R. aureum
Robinia hispida
Rosa centifolia muscosa
  R. semperflorens var.
  R. 'Slaters' Crimson'
  R. s. 'Parsons' Pink'
  R. odorata
  R. rugosa
  R. multiflora
  R. m. platyphylla
  R. pimpinella
  R. rubrifolia
Rubus odoratus
  R. biflorus
Salix babylonica
Sambucus nigra viridis
  S. n. aurea-variegata
  S. n. alba-variegata
  S. n. pulverentula
  S. canadensis
Saphora japonica
Spiraea tomontosa
  S. douglasii
  S. crenata
  S. chamaedryfolia
Symphoricarpos orbiculatus
  S. rivularis

Syringa x *rothomagensis*
Ulex europeus (double)
Veronica elliptica
Vitis vimifera 'Incana'
Wisteria fruticosa

W. sinensis
Yucca aloifolia
   Y. recurvifolia
   Y. glauca
   Y. flaccida

VICTORIAN
FLOWERS

Alchemilla mollis
Alstroemeria aurantiaca
Anemone japonica
   A. vitifolia
   A. x *elegans*
   A. nemorosa allenii
   A. robinsoniana
Aquilegia coerulea
   A. chrysantha
Astilbe thunbergii
Brachycome iberidifolia
Caltha polypetala
Camassia esculenta
   C. leichtlinii
Chionodoxa luciliae
   C. sardensis
Clarkia elegans
Colchicum speciosum
Dahlia (Cactus, Show and
   Pompon types especially)
Dicentra spectabilis
Erigeron macranthus
   E. aurantiacus
Gaillardia amblyodon
Gladiolus, Ghent hybrids
   G. brenchleyensis
   G. lemonii
   G. primulinus
Helleborus orientalis
   H. guttatus
   H. odorus
   H. corsicus
Hemerocallis kwanso
Hosta fortunei

Hyacinthus azureus
Impatiens roylei
Ipomoea purga
Iris unguicularis
Lilium auratum
   L. speciosum
   L. testaceum
Linaria marocanna
Lychnis coeli-rosa oculata
Meconopsis quintuplinervia
Mimulus cupreus
   M. cardinalis
Narcissus exertus ornatus
   N. 'Poetaz' (types)
   N. cyclameneus
   N. triandrus
Nemophyla insignis
Nerine bowdenii
Oenothera erythrosepala
   O. whitneyi
Peltiphyllum pellatum
Penstemon hartwegii
   P. cobaea
Petunia nyetaginiflora
   P. violacea
Phlox drummondii
Physalis alkekengi
Platycodon grandiflorum
   mariesii
Primula denticulata
   P. japonica
   P. sikkimensis
Salvia patens
   S. farinacea

Saxifraga granulata tricolor
   S. fortunei
   S. purpurescens
Sedum spectabile
Tagetes petula nana

Tropaeolum speciosum
Tulipa kaufmanniana
Verbena x *hybrida*
Viola, 'Fancy Pansies', 'Viola'
   types and 'Violettas'.

TREES AND SHRUBS

Abelia chinensis
   A. uniflora
   A. floribunda
Acer palmatum
Actinidia chinensis
   A. kolomikta
Arundinaria japonica
   A. nitida
   A. fastuosa
Berberidopsis corallina
Berberis darwinii
   B. stenophylla
   B. thunbergii
Buddleia davidii
   B. colvilei
   B. lindlyana
   B. auriculata
Calycanthus occidentalis
Camellia donckelarii
   C. sasanqua
Campsis x *tagliabuana*
Carpenteria californica
Caryopteris mongholica
   C. mastacanthus
Cedrus deodara
Ceonothus thrysiflorus
   C. dentatus floribundus
   C. x *veitchianus*
   C. x *lobbianus*
   C. x *delilianus*
Ceratostigma plumbaginoides
Chaenomeles japonica
Chamaecyparis lawsoniana
Cistus loretti
Clematis montana
   C. patens

   C. lanuginosa
   C. hendersonii
   C. x *reginae*
   C. x *jackmanii*
   C. tangutica
Cornus alba sibirica
   C. a. atrosanguinea
   C. a. flaviramea
   C. nuttallii
   C. kousa
Cotoneaster horizontalis
   C. franchetii
   C. bullatus
Crinodendron hookerianum
Cupressus macrocarpa
Cytisus scoparius
   andreanus
   C. dallimerii
   C. x *verisicolor*
   C. x *praecox*
Daphne genka
   D. creanata fl. pl.
   D. candissima
   D. 'Pride of Rochester'
   D. gracilis
   D. purpurescens
   D. x *rosea*
Desfontainea spinosa
Diervilla florida
   D. coraeensis
   D. japonica
   D. praecox
   D. middendorffiana
   D. x 'Abel Carriere'
   D. x 'Van Houttei'
   D. x *loomansii aurea*

Eleagnus multiflora
  E. pungens
  E. p. variegata
  E. macrophylla
  E. glabra
Embothrium coccineum
Enkianthus campanulatus
Erica darleyensis
Escallonia rubra
  E. illinita
  E. organensis
  E. pterocladon
  E. macrantha
  E. virgata
  E. x *exoniensis*
  E. x *langleyensis*
  E. x *edinensis*
  E. x *balfourii*
Eucryphia glutinosa
  E. cordifolia
Euonymus fortunei
Fatsia japonica
Forsythia suspensa
  F. viridissima
  F. x *intermedia* vars.
Fuchsia fulgens
  F. magellanica discolor
  F. m. riccartonii
  F. m. pumila
  F. m. thomsonii
Garrya elliptica
Gunnera chilensis
Hamamelis japonica
  arborea
  H. mollis
Hedera colchica
Hibiscus 'Coeleste'
  H. 'Totus Albus'
Hydrangea paniculata
  H. p. grandiflora
  H. p. floribunda
  H. petiolaris
  H. japonica
  H. acuminata
  H. thunbergii

Hypericum patulum
  H. p. henryi
  H. x *moserianum*
  H. hookerianum
  H. h. 'Rogersii'
  H. leschenaultii
Jasminum officinale affine
  J. nudiflorum
Kerria japonica
Ligustrum sinense
  L. quihoui
  L. japonica
  rotundifolium
Lonicera japonica
  aureoreticulata
  L. fragrantissima
  L. standishii
  L. syringantha
Magnolia stellata
  M. s. 'Rosea'
  M. sieboldii
Mahonia undulata
  M. japonica
  M. bealei
  M. napaulensis
Myrtus ugni
Olearia haastii
  O. gunniana
  O. macrodonta
Osmanthus ilicifolius
  O. delavayi
Paeonia lutea
  P. delaveyi
  P. x *lemoinei*
Parthenocissus tricuspidata
  P. vitacea
Pernettya mucronata
  angustifolia
Philadelphus coulteri
  P. microphyllus
  P. x *lemoinei*
  P. x *purpureo-maculatus*
Phillyrea decora
Phyllostachys henonis
  P. mitis

Pieris japonica
  P. formosa
Polygonum baldschuanicum
Ponciris trifoliata
Prunus triloba
  P. cerasifera pissardii
Pyracantha coccinea lalandei
Rhododendron ciliatum
  R. campylocarpum
  R. falconieri
  R. cinnarbarinum
  R. thompsonii
  R. griffithianum
  R. fortunei
  R. x *praecox*
  R. japonicum
  R. occidentale
  R. 'Kurume' azaleas
Rhus cotinoides (Cotinus coggyrea)
Ribes sanguineum 'Splendens'
  R. x *gordonianum*
  R. speciosum
Romneya coulteri
Rosa wichuriana
Rubus deliciosus
  R. spectabilis
  R. parviflorus
  R. phoenicolasius
Sarcococca saligna
  S. hookeriana
Sasa tessilata
Sequoia wellingtonia

Skimmia japonica
  S. reevesiana
Spiraea menziesii
  S. japonica
  S. j. 'Anthony Waterer'
  S. bullata
  S. prunifolia fl. pl.
  S. thunbergii
  S. 'Van Houttei'
Staphylea colchica
  S. x *coulombierii*
Styrax obassia
Syringa josikaea
  S. emodi
  S. oblata
  S. villosa
  S. x *henryii*
Tamarix tetrandra
Veronica hulkeana
  V. speciosa
  V. brachysiphon
  V. anomala
  V. cupressoides
Viburnum macrocephalum
  V. tomentosum plicatum
  V. t. x *mariesii*
Vitis amurensis
  V. davidii
  V. thunbergii
  V. coignetiae
  V. flexuosa
Wisteria floribunda macrobotrys

10
Gardens with period features

The following gardens contain features of the period indicated and frequently of other periods too. An indication of particular features of interest or of persons associated with the garden is given in some cases. In other cases the garden is an interesting example of the style of the period. Although most of these gardens are open to the public at certain times this is not invariably the case.

Medieval gardens
Kenilworth Castle, Warwickshire: pleasance.
Newstead Abbey, Nottinghamshire: fishponds.

Tudor gardens
Boscobel House, Shropshire: mount.
Dunham Massey, Greater Manchester: mount.
Haddon Hall, Derbyshire: terraced gardens.
Hampton Court, London: restored knot gardens and privy garden.
New College, Oxford: mount.
Northbourne Court, Kent: mount, sunken garden.
Wadham College, Oxford: mount.

Stuart and early Georgian gardens
Basing House, Hampshire: restored parterre.
Blickling Hall, Norfolk: allées through woodland.
Bramham Park, West Yorkshire: allées through woodland.
Edzell Castle, Tayside: garden walls, knot garden.
Grimsthorpe Castle, Lincolnshire: formal bastioned garden.
Ham House, London: restored wilderness, formal gardens.
Hampton Court, London: fountain garden, canal.
Hardwick Hall, Derbyshire: garden walls and gateways.
Levens Hall, Cumbria: topiary.
Melbourne Hall, Derbyshire: parterre, allées through woodland.
Packwood House, Warwickshire: topiary.
Powis Castle, Powys: terraced garden.
St Pauls Walden Bury, Hertfordshire: allées through woodland.
Westbury Court, Gloucestershire: canals.

English landscape gardens
Attingham Park, Shropshire: Repton.
Belton House, Lincolnshire: William Emes.
Blenheim Palace, Oxfordshire: Brown.
Bowood, Wiltshire: Brown.
Burghley Park, Cambridgeshire: Brown.

Castle Howard, North Yorkshire: Vanbrugh.
Chiswick House, London: Kent.
Claremont, Surrey: Vanbrugh, Bridgeman, Kent.
Clumber Park, Nottinghamshire.
Croome Court, Worcestershire: Brown.
Duncombe Park, North Yorkshire: terrace walk.
Hagley Hall, Worcestershire: Sanderson Miller.
Harewood House, West Yorkshire: Brown.
Holkham Hall, Norfolk: Repton.
The Leasowes, West Midlands: William Shenstone.
Painshill Park, Surrey: Charles Hamilton.
Petworth House, West Sussex: Brown.
Rousham House, Oxfordshire: Kent.
Sheringham Hall, Norfolk: Repton.
Stourhead, Wiltshire: the second Henry Hoare.
Stowe, Buckinghamshire: Vanbrugh, Kent, Brown.
Studley Royal, North Yorkshire.
West Wycombe, Buckinghamshire.
Wimpole Hall, Cambridgeshire: Brown.

Nineteenth-century gardens
Abbey Park, Leicester: William Barron.
Battersea Park, London: James Pennethorne.
Belsay, Northumberland.
Biddulph Grange, Staffordshire: James Bateman.
Birkenhead Park, Merseyside: Sir Joseph Paxton.

55. The garden at Chiswick House was planned around the villa of Lord Burlington and was the work of William Kent.

NINETEENTH-CENTURY GARDENS

Birmingham Botanic Gardens, West Midlands.
Bodnant, Gwynedd: Lord Aberconwy.
Bowood, Wiltshire: Brown.
Chatsworth, Derbyshire: Sir Joseph Paxton.
Cliveden, Buckinghamshire.
Cragside, Northumberland.
Derby Arboretum, Derbyshire: J. C. Loudon, earliest public park designed as such.
Edinburgh, Royal Botanic Garden.
Elvaston Castle, Derbyshire: William Barron.
Harewood House, West Yorkshire: Sir Charles Barry.
Heligan, Cornwall: the Lost Gardens.
Hever Castle, Kent.
Hughenden Manor, Buckinghamshire.
Inverewe, Wester Ross, Highland: Osgood Mackenzie.
Kew, Royal Botanic Garden, London.
Killerton House, Devon.
Lochinch and Castle Kennedy, Dumfries and Galloway: sub-tropical.
Muncaster Castle, Cumbria.
Prince's Park, Liverpool: Sir Joseph Paxton.
Sefton Park, Liverpool: Edouard André, Lewis Hornblower.

56. Part of the parterre based on an eighteenth-century French design on the main lawn at Cliveden.

Shrubland Park, Suffolk: Sir Charles Barry.
Swiss Garden, Old Warden, Bedfordshire: picturesque.
Thoresby Hall, Nottinghamshire: formal bedding.
Trentham Gardens, Staffordshire: Sir Charles Barry.
Tresco, Isles of Scilly: sub-tropical.
Victoria Park, London: James Pennethorne.
Westonbirt, Gloucestershire: tree and shrub collection.
Wilton House, Wiltshire.

Twentieth-century gardens
Anglesey Abbey, Cambridgeshire: Lord Fairhaven.
Buscot Park, Oxfordshire: Harold Peto.
Exbury Gardens, Hampshire: Lionel de Rothschild.
Folly Farm, Berkshire: Gertrude Jekyll, Sir Edwin Lutyens.
Gravetye, West Sussex: William Robinson.
Harlow Carr Botanic Garden, Harrogate, North Yorkshire: Northern
    Horticultural Society.
Hemel Hempstead, Hertfordshire: water gardens in town centre by
    Sir Geoffrey Jellicoe.
Hestercombe, Taunton, Somerset: Gertrude Jekyll, Sir Edwin
    Lutyens.
Hever Castle, Kent: F. L. Pearson, Joseph Cheal.
Hidcote Manor, Gloucestershire: Lawrence Johnston.
Iford Manor, Wiltshire: Harold Peto.
Lea Rhododendron Gardens, Derbyshire.
Nymans, West Sussex: Gertrude Jekyll.
Savill Garden, Windsor Great Park, Berkshire: Sir Eric Savill.
Sheffield Park, East Sussex: tree and shrub collection, Arthur Soames.
Sissingshurst Castle, Kent: Sir Harold Nicolson and Victoria
    Sackville-West.
Wakehurst Place, West Sussex: woodland garden.
Wisley Garden, Surrey: Royal Horticultural Society.

11
Some period gardens to visit

The following notes describe a selection of the gardens made in Britain during recent years in the style of gardens of the past. All are regularly open to the public and telephone numbers are given so that opening times can be checked prior to making a visit.

Audley End House, Saffron Walden, Essex CB11 4JF. Telephone: 01799 522399. English Heritage.

The great Jacobean house is surrounded by a large landscape park, but close to the house much work has been done recently to recreate the effect of the formal gardens which once existed here, including a large parterre.

Biddulph Grange, Biddulph, Stoke-on-Trent, Staffordshire ST8 7SD. Telephone: 01782 517999. National Trust.

The garden made by James Bateman and Edward Cooke between 1846 and 1871 has a number of distinct areas each devoted to exotic styles of gardening. It has been recently restored by the National Trust.

57. At Audley End in Essex English Heritage have recreated an early nineteenth-century parterre.

58. The Entrance to Egypt is one of the garden features at Biddulph Grange.

Blenheim Palace, Woodstock, Oxford OX7 1PX. Telephone: 01993 811325.

The east garden, below the private apartments of the Duke of Marlborough, is a parterre with scrollwork in box accentuated by pink roses and topiary and by large pots of flowers. In the centre is a mermaid fountain. It was designed by the French landscape architect Achille Duchêne in 1908 in restoration of the earlier flower garden on the same site which had been swept away by Lancelot Brown in the 1760s. The west, or water, gardens were made in the 1920s also by Duchêne on lines suggested by Vanbrugh when he was building the palace but never carried out at that time. Both gardens are on the grandest scale, as befits a ducal residence, with swirling patterns set out in box in the east garden and numerous pools, fountains, statuary and topiary in the water gardens.

Castle Bromwich Hall Gardens, Chester Road, Castle Bromwich, West Midlands B36 9BT. Telephone: 0121-749 4100.

The formal gardens of the seventeenth and eighteenth centuries around the house of 1657 are still under restoration but a maze, orangery, cold bath and holly walk may be seen. Planting is strictly in period.

Christ Church Cathedral, Oxford OX1 1DP. Telephone: 01865 276150.

Part of the original cloister garth has been planted as a late medieval garden to a design prepared by Mavis Batey. There are raised beds, a trellis fence and potted carnations. It is open when the cathedral is open.

Cressing Temple, Witham Road, Braintree, Essex CM7 8PD. Telephone: 01376 584903.

A garden of generally Tudor style has been created within the walled garden of this moated farmstead. The garden is one of the features of the exhibition on the history of the place which is open to the public.

Eastbury Manor House, Barking, Essex IG11 9SN. Telephone: 0181-507 0119. National Trust.

The garden of this medium-sized Elizabethan house is being recreated in sympathy with the house. The garden is in four sections and these are gradually being restored.

Edzell Castle, Brechin, Tayside, Scotland. Telephone: 01356 648631. Historic Scotland.

The ruined wings of this tower house enclose a courtyard with elaborately sculptured walls. They are embellished with panels of

59. At Cressing Temple the knot garden, arbour and meadow beyond are enclosed within a walled garden.

60. The Elizabethan Gardens, Plymouth, have a pond and small knot garden fitted in among the remains of old buildings. Beyond can be seen the rose garden planted with old-fashioned roses.

sculpture and boxes for flowers (or possibly nesting boxes for birds). The original design of the actual garden within these walls is unknown but an appropriately designed knot garden has been created which contrasts pleasantly with the shattered buildings of the castle.

The Elizabethan Gardens, 12/14 Royal Parade, Plymouth, Devon PL1 1DT. Telephone: 01752 661161.

A series of four small, enclosed gardens was laid out in 1970 on derelict land by the Plymouth Barbican Association in commemoration of the 350th anniversary of the sailing of the *Mayflower*. Designed by Alan Miller-Williams with horticultural advice from Mrs Iris Webb, the gardens comprise a lawn garden, a water garden with pool of formal shape, a knot garden with box hedging and a rose garden planted with old-fashioned roses. The gardens are approached from either New Street or Castle Street.

Elvaston Castle, Elvaston Castle Country Park, Thulston, Derby DE7 3EP. Telephone: 01332 863822.

The gardens date mainly from the 1840s and are open to the public as a country park. Following years of neglect the restoration

61. Fishbourne Roman Palace has a demonstration garden of plants known to have been grown in Roman Britain.

work has included much remedial treatment of the extensive exotic evergreen planting. Close to the house an elaborate formal area, beyond restoration, has been replaced by a large new parterre in box.

Fishbourne Roman Palace, Salthill Road, Chichester, West Sussex PO19 3QR. Telephone: 01243 785869.

Although there is no evidence that the remarkable so-called Roman Palace was ever known as such to its builders, it is undoubtedly palatial in size and elaboration. The development of the palace was complex, but by about AD 75 it comprised a large rectangle of buildings within which was a formal garden. From the large entrance hall in the centre of the east wing there extended a wide pathway, lined by hedges, across the garden to the audience chamber in the centre of the west wing. Much of this garden has been recreated and replanted using plants usual in Roman gardens, although no direct evidence survives to show exactly which plants were there originally. There is a garden in a corner of the site displaying plants known to have been grown in Roman Britain.

Gainsborough Old Hall, Parnell Street, Gainsborough, Lincolnshire DN21 2NB. Telephone: 01427 612669.

The Old Hall, on the north side of the town centre, is a late medieval brick-built manor house. In the courtyard a small garden

62. One of the sunken gardens in seventeenth-century style at Hampton Court, reconstructed on the site of one of the original Tudor gardens.

has been laid out with raised beds planted with plants which would have been available in the 1470s to Sir Thomas Burgh, the builder of the Old Hall.

Hampton Court Palace, East Molesey, London KT8 9AH. Telephone: 0181-781 9787. Historic Royal Palaces.

The great palace of Wolsey, Henry VIII and William and Mary is surrounded by gardens, the largest of which is the Great Fountain Garden on the east side of the palace. This is rather more a survival than a restoration, although some replanting of the limes has been carried out in recent years. On the south side of the palace the Privy Garden has recently been reconstructed and replanted, restoring it

63. The restored Privy Garden at Hampton Court.

to its 1702 layout, in the most spectacular garden restoration scheme of recent years. To the west of the Privy Garden is a small knot garden designed by Ernest Law in 1924 as an example of the kind of garden which must have existed here in Tudor times. There are also two small sunken gardens which are derived from traces of the original Tudor gardens but were redesigned in the eighteenth century.

Hanbury Hall, Droitwich, Worcestershire WR9 7EA. Telephone: 01527 84214. National Trust.

The gardens laid out by Thomas Vernon, possibly to the designs of George London, when he remodelled his house early in the eighteenth century, were all swept away less than a century later. They are now being restored with the aid of a bird's eye drawing of 1732, and now the parterre to the west of the house can be seen once more. It appears never to have been directly aligned with the house and this and other oddities are being retained in the restoration.

Hatfield House, Hatfield, Hertfordshire AL9 5NF. Telephone: 01707 262823.

The gardens around the great house built by Robert Cecil early in the seventeenth century fell into decay in later centuries but have been recreated. The lower West Garden was replanted as long ago as 1900 with scented plants and herbs. One mulberry remains of the four planted by James I. The East Garden is planted mainly with herbaceous plants and the terraces have been recently restored. The courtyard of the Old Palace is now a scented knot garden with many plants known to have been grown by John Tradescant, gardener here in the seventeenth century. The maze, on a further terrace below the East Garden, is planted in box.

Herterton House, Hartington, Cambo, Morpeth, Northumberland NE61 4BN. Telephone: 0167 074 278.

The garden here is a recent recreation of a small country house garden in the formal manner of the seventeenth and eighteenth centuries. There is a small topiary garden, a herb or physic garden growing ancient medicinal, economic and aromatic plants, a flower garden with a good collection of herbaceous plants, including many old selections of uncommon forms of wild plants, a foliage 'maze' garden and a nursery selling a selection of the plants grown.

Hertford Museum, 18 Bull Plain, Hertford SG14 1DT. Telephone: 01992 582686.

The museum building dates back to 1610 and a garden has been laid out to display typical features of an early seventeenth-century town garden. There is a knot garden, beds surrounded by balus-

64. Seventeenth-century knot garden designs have been set in the lawn at Kenilworth Castle.

trades, an arbour, a camomile seat and a bee shelter. Planting is of plants available during the period. It is accessible to the disabled.

Kenilworth Castle, Kenilworth, Warwickshire. Telephone: 01926 852078. English Heritage.

Just to the north of the keep of the magnificent castle the Tudor Garden has been reconstructed along the lines of a seventeenth-century plan. Only the outlines of the beds have been set out in box. Originally sage, lavender and other herbs would have filled up the beds in place of the grass which is there now.

King John's Garden, Church Street, Romsey, Hampshire SO51 8BT. Telephone: 01794 512200.

King John's House is a thirteenth-century building now open as a heritage centre. Although the site of this small garden once belonged to the Romsey Nunnery no records survive to indicate whether the land was a garden. Later occupied by cottages, some walls of which remain, the garden is intended as a suitable setting for the ancient buildings around it, with a flower garden of medieval inspiration and a small herb garden. It is still under development, with much depending on voluntary labour.

Kirby Hall, Deene, near Corby, Northamptonshire NN17 3EN. Telephone: 01536 203230. English Heritage.

The Great Garden of 1685-6 has been the subject of extensive archaeological investigation prior to the recreation of the northern part of the garden. Originally the layout extended much further south and included a formal wilderness. Reconstruction is in progress.

Little Moreton Hall, Congleton, Cheshire CW12 4SP. Telephone: 01260 272018. National Trust.

There are no records of the original gardens of this fifteenth-century manor house and some twenty years ago the knot garden was laid out in dwarf box with gravel and grass, based on a design in Leonard Meager's *The Complete English Gardener* of 1670. The side beds have herbaceous plants of the period. The Elizabethan house is now complemented by hedged enclosures, and there is an orchard with traditional varieties of quinces, medlars and apples.

Llancaiach Fawr, Nelson, Treharris, Glamorgan CF46 6ER. Telephone: 01443 412248.

The semi-fortified Llancaiach Fawr Manor was built about 1530 and is now a living history museum. In 1645 Charles I visited the owner and the museum seeks to convey an idea of what it was like to live there during the Civil War period. The reconstructed garden is among the exhibits.

The Master's Garden, Lord Leycester Hospital, High Street, Warwick CV34 4BH. Telephone: 01926 491422 or 492797.

There has been a garden to the rear of the half-timbered build-

65. The reconstructed knot garden at Little Moreton Hall.

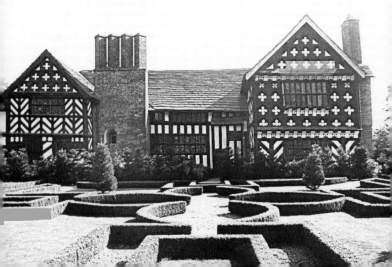

66. The knot garden at Moseley Old Hall, near Wolverhampton, laid out by the National Trust. The design is copied from a seventeenth-century plan with plants characteristic of the middle of that century.

ings, founded as a home for twelve old soldiers, for almost five hundred years. Closed for many years, the garden has recently been restored under the supervision of Geoffrey Smith, with the assistance of detailed accounts dating back to the 1660s.

Moseley Old Hall, Fordhouses, Wolverhampton, West Midlands WV10 7HY. Telephone: 01902 782808. National Trust.

This house, some four miles north of Wolverhampton, is of Elizabethan origin, though later encased in brick. Here Charles II hid during his flight after the battle of Worcester in 1651. It came into the care of the National Trust in 1962 with virtually no garden save a few old trees. The Trust therefore created a garden of a type characteristic of the period when the house made its brief entry into history in 1651. The garden comprises a knot garden which is a copy of one designed by the Reverend Walter Stonehouse at Darfield in 1640. The pattern is set out in box with different colours of gravels used to emphasise the pattern and along one side is a walk covered with a timber arbour on which are trained clematis and the Tienturier grape. There is a nut walk leading to the gate through which Charles is traditionally said to have come from the fields to

67. The garden laid out in seventeenth-century style by the Tradescant Trust in part of the churchyard of St Mary's, Lambeth. The church has been adapted as a museum of garden history.

seek refuge in the house. A herb garden and an orchard complete the garden and all the plants used, save possibly some of the trees in the new orchard, are ones in cultivation in the mid seventeenth century.

Museum of Garden History, St Mary-at-Lambeth, Lambeth Palace Road, London SE1 7JU. Telephone: 0171-373 4030.

The church, close to the gates of Lambeth Palace, was closed for worship in 1972. The decaying building was rescued in 1979 by the Tradescant Trust, a voluntary organisation formed for the purpose, who have adapted it as a museum of garden history. There is a display on the John Tradescants, father and son, the pioneer gardeners of the early seventeenth century. In the churchyard a period garden has been created, designed by Mary Searls, John Drake and Lady Salisbury of Hatfield House, where the elder Tradescant was once a gardener. There is a knot garden and all the plants are either known to have been grown by the Tradescants or are of the period. The plants were the gifts of nurserymen through-out Britain and the garden is maintained by voluntary labour. Amid the garden is the tomb of the two Tradescants as well as that of Captain Bligh of *Bounty* fame.

Painswick Rococo Garden, Painswick, Gloucestershire GL6 6TH. Telephone: 01452 813204.

A rare example of the eighteenth-century taste for rococo in garden design is in course of restoration under the guidance of Paul Edwards using the paintings of the garden by Thomas Robins of 1748.

68. *The early eighteenth-century garden at Painswick, Gloucestershire, now has an exedra as part of the current restoration. Paintings by Thomas Robins showing the garden as it was in the mid eighteenth century have assisted the restoration scheme.*

Pallant House, 9 North Pallant, Chichester, West Sussex PO19 1TJ. Telephone: 01243 774557.

The house dates from 1712 and has been restored as an art gallery as well as an historic house. To the rear, what was until recently a yard has been redesigned by Claude Phillimore as a notional reconstruction of a typical small garden of a town house of the mid eighteenth century. The original garden was much larger but no evidence of its design has survived. In the small space available now there is box hedging, standard honeysuckles and many other plants available to eighteenth-century gardeners. Trellis with ivy has been used to mask the awkward shape of the garden. It is open when the house is open.

Pickford's House Museum, 41 Friargate, Derby DE1 1DA. Telephone: 01332 255363.

Joseph Pickford, an architect, built his house at 41 Friargate in 1770 and it has been opened as a small museum of social history. Although it is known that there was a garden, no records survive to indicate the design. A new garden in the style of an eighteenth-century town garden was made by Derbyshire College of Agriculture and Horticulture and completed in 1991. Planting is of plants available by 1770 but choice has been restricted by the overshadowing of neighbouring buildings. It is open when the museum is open.

Pitmedden, Udny, Aberdeen, Grampian. Telephone: 01651 842352. National Trust for Scotland.

When the Pitmedden estate was presented to the National Trust for Scotland in 1952 the Trust decided to restore the Great Garden which had been made by Sir Alexander Seton in the seventeenth century. The work was commenced in 1956 and has resulted in a walled garden with parterres and two garden pavilions with ogee-shaped roofs. The designs for three of the four parterres are based upon those shown at the Palace of Holyroodhouse in the bird's eye view of Edinburgh in 1647 by James Gordon of Rothiemay. The fourth parterre is based on Sir Alexander Seton's coat of arms. They are set out in box, coloured pebbles and bedding plants.

Queen Eleanor's Garden, Winchester Castle, Winchester, Hampshire. Telephone: 01962 841841.

In a confined site behind the Great Hall of the castle a garden in the style typical of the thirteenth century has been created to a design by Dr Sylvia Landsberg. The planting is of the period and the fountain and seats are based upon remains at Winchester. Open at the same time as the castle, it is reached through the Great Hall.

69. The garden of Red Lodge, Bristol. The late sixteenth-century house is now a museum and this knot garden has been reconstructed on the site of part of the once more extensive gardens.

The Queen's Garden, Royal Botanic Gardens, Kew, Richmond, London TW9 3AB. Telephone: 0181-940 1171.

The garden was made from a patch of waste ground behind the small seventeenth-century palace and was opened by Her Majesty The Queen in 1969. The main area is occupied by a parterre but there is also a sunken garden surrounded by a pleached alley of laburnum and with a turf seat. A mount has been converted from a heap of furnace ash and is surmounted by a rotunda. The arcaded loggia has been replaced at the back of the palace to provide a suitable link with the garden.

Red Lodge, Park Row, Bristol BS1 5LJ. Telephone: 0117-929 9771.

The Red Lodge is a branch museum of the City Museum and Art Gallery and is the only remaining building of a small estate which, at the end of the sixteenth century, included the 'Great House' on the site now occupied by the Colston Hall. The gardens then included the Red and White Lodges and eight walled gardens extended down the hill. The garden which was laid out to the rear of the Red Lodge in 1984 is generally of early seventeenth-century design with a knot garden in box based on a plasterwork design on the ceiling of one of the bedrooms. Around this are beds of herbaceous plants, and the walls and trellis support espaliered fruit trees, roses, honeysuckle, jasmine and vines. The garden is designed to be seen from above, as were so many gardens of the period, and from the windows of the house – and the adjacent multi-storey car park – a fine view is obtained.

The Royal Pavilion, Brighton, East Sussex BN1 1EE. Telephone: 01273 603005.

The surroundings of the Prince Regent's extraordinary pleasure palace have recently been transformed to recreate something of the splendours of the Regency garden which once existed on the west side of the building. Planting has been designed to be in period and the plants are ones which would have been familiar to the Regent.

The Shakespearian gardens, Shakespeare Birthplace Trust, Stratford-upon-Avon, Warwickshire. Telephone: 01789 204016.

The buildings preserved by the Shakespeare Birthplace Trust all have associated gardens which form a suitable setting. These are mostly simple affairs, planted with plants mentioned in the plays, but at New Place, where the poet spent his brief retirement, the Trust laid out an Elizabethan garden on the site which must have been occupied by the poet's own garden. Designed by Ernest Law and constructed in 1912-21, it is enclosed by an oak palisade and tunnel covered with crab apple. The four knots are set out in box, savory, hyssop, lavender cotton, thyme and other herbs with the spaces filled with flowers. The Great Garden, adjoining to the south along Chapel Lane, is on the site of the poet's orchard and kitchen garden. Here the long borders are treated formally in the Tudor manner with divisions of yew hedging. An aged mulberry is reputed to have been grown from a cutting from a tree of Stratford's greatest son.

Swiss Garden, Old Warden, near Biggleswade, Bedfordshire. Telephone: 01234 228330.

The picturesque garden created by Robert, third Lord Ongley, in the 1820s has been carefully restored by Bedfordshire County Council following a long period of neglect. At the centre is the thatched Swiss Cottage on its rounded hill and there is a tufa grotto which leads into a fernery beneath a glass and iron roof. There are many fine trees which survive from the original planting.

Tretower Court, Crickhowell, Powys NP8 2RF. Telephone: 01874 730279. Cadw, Welsh Historic Monuments.

The courtyard house was remodelled by Sir Roger Vaughan in

the fifteenth century but there is no direct evidence of the garden he must have laid out then. A garden of the kind which would be expected of a wealthy, and much travelled, commoner has recently been laid out to the south of the house. There are turf seats, a tunnel arbour and a small pavilion. Planting is authentic for the period with vines, lilies and irises and there is much trellis supporting honeysuckles.

Tudor House Museum, Bugle Street, Southampton SO1 0AD. Telephone: 01703 332513.

To the rear of the museum, a large town house of the early Tudor period, a garden has been constructed to designs by Dr Sylvia Landsberg which shows small examples of large garden features of the period. The general effect is probably more elaborate than would have been that of a real garden of the Tudor period because of the relatively small area but the many distinctive features shown make this garden specially instructive, and appropriate for a museum garden. Thus there will be found here an arbour, covered walks, heraldic ornaments and rails painted white and green, a knot garden and a secret garden one peers into to see a bee skep in a niche in the wall. The plants have been carefully selected from those available in the sixteenth century.

70. At the Weald and Downland Open Air Museum, Singleton, Sussex, the garden of Bayleaf Farmstead has been reconstructed as it might have been during the early sixteenth century.

Weald and Downland Open Air Museum, Singleton, Chichester, West Sussex PO18 0EU. Telephone: 01243 811348.

Bayleaf Farmstead forms part of this museum of buildings transported from elsewhere in south-eastern England and re-erected here. Around the farmhouse is a garden of the type which would have been found about 1540 belonging to a yeoman. At this social level the garden was largely utilitarian rather than ornamental, although there are a few roses, and a wattle-edged bed of herbs. The vegetable garden occupies most of the space, with six plots divided by paths wide enough for a barrow. Around the garden is a wattled hazel pole fence. There are bee hives in the shade of a plum tree. The general effect may well strike the twentieth-century visitor as untidy, but our ancestors placed less stress on orderly maintenance than we do today.

West Dean Gardens, West Dean, Chichester, West Sussex PO18 0QZ. Telephone: 01243 811303.

The house, now West Dean College, is surrounded by a 'picturesque' park, but the walled gardens are now of great interest, being that rarest type of surviving period garden, a kitchen garden. Here can be seen in full working order the frame yard with glasshouses, the nursery yard, and the pit yard with hot beds. The fruit garden has a crinkle-crankle wall.

71. The walled gardens of West Dean, Sussex, are now restored as a rare example of the great kitchen gardens of the Edwardian period.

12
Further reading

Anthony, John. *The Renaissance Garden in Britain*. Shire, 1991.
Banks, Elizabeth. *Creating Period Gardens*. Phaidon Press, 1991.
Batey, Mavis. *Regency Gardens*. Shire, 1995.
Batey, Mavis, and Lambert, David. *The English Garden Tour*. Murray, 1990.
Bisgrove, Richard. *The English Garden*. Viking, 1990.
Brown, Jane. *The Art and Architecture of English Gardens*. Weidenfeld & Nicolson, 1989.
Campbell, Susan. *Charleston Kedding, a History of Kitchen Gardening*. Ebury Press, 1996.
Chadwick, G. F. *The Park and the Town, Public Landscape in the 19th and 20th Centuries*. Architectural Press, 1966.
Clark, Frank. *The English Landscape Garden*. Pleiades Books, 1948; Alan Sutton, 1980.
Coats, Alice M. *Flowers and Their Histories*. Hulton Press, 1956.
Coats, Alice M. *Garden Shrubs and Their Histories*. Studio Vista, 1963.
Coats, Alice M. *The Quest for Plants: A History of the Horticultural Explorers*. Phoenix House, 1968.
Desmond, Ray. *Bibliography of British Gardens*. St Paul's Bibliographies, 1984; revised 1990.
Duthie, Ruth. *Florists' Flowers and Societies*. Shire, 1989.
Edwards, Paul. *English Garden Ornament*. Bell, 1965.
Elliott, Brent. *Victorian Gardens*. Batsford, 1986.
George, Michael, and Bowe, Patrick. *The Gardens of Ireland*. Hutchinson, 1986.
Goode, Patrick, and Lancaster, Michael (editors). *The Oxford Companion to Gardens*. Oxford University Press, 1986.
Green, David. *Gardener to Queen Anne: Henry Wise and the Formal Garden*. Oxford University Press, 1956.
Hadfield, Miles. *A History of British Gardening*. Spring Books, 1969; John Murray, 1979. (Originally published as *Gardening in Britain*, Hutchinson, 1960.)
Hadfield, Miles. *The English Landscape Garden*. Shire, second edition, reprinted 1997.
Harris, John. *The Artist and the Country House*. Sotheby, 1979; revised 1985.
Harvey, John. *Early Gardening Catalogues*. Phillimore, 1972.
Harvey, John. *Early Nurserymen*. Phillimore, 1974.
Harvey, John. *Medieval Gardens*. Batsford, 1981.
Harvey, John. *The Availability of Plants of the Late Eighteenth*

Century. Garden History Society, 1988.

Harvey, John. *Restoring Period Gardens*. Shire, second edition 1993.

Hix, John. *The Glass House*. Phaidon, 1974.

Hobhouse, Penelope. *Plants in Garden History*. Pavilion, 1992.

Hunt, John Dixon. *Garden and Grove: the Italian Renaissance Garden in the English Imagination, 1600-1750*. Dent, 1987.

Hunt, John Dixon, and Willis, Peter (editors). *The Genius of the Place: the English Landscape Garden, 1620-1820*. Paul Elek, 1975; revised edition MIT, 1989. (Anthology.)

Hunt, Peter. *The Shell Gardens Book*. Phoenix House, 1964.

Hunt, Peter. *The Book of Garden Ornament*. Dent, 1974.

Hussey, Christopher. *English Gardens and Landscapes 1700-1750*. Country Life, 1967.

Hussey, Christopher. *The Picturesque*. 1927; Frank Cass, 1967.

Huxley, Anthony. *An Illustrated History of Gardening*. Paddington Press, 1978.

Jacques, David. *Georgian Gardens*. Batsford, 1983.

Jacques, David, and van der Horst, Arend. *The Gardens of William and Mary*. Croom Helm, 1988.

Jellicoe, Sir Geoffrey and Susan. *The Landscape of Man*. Thames & Hudson, 1975.

Jones, Barbara. *Follies and Grottoes*. Constable, 1974.

Leith-Ross, Prudence. *The John Tradescants*. Owen, 1984.

Lemmon, Kenneth. *The Covered Garden*. Museum Press, 1962.

Malins, Edward. *English Landscaping and Literature, 1660-1840*. Oxford University Press, 1966.

Malins, Edward, and The Knight of Glin. *Lost Demesnes: Irish Landscape Gardening 1660-1845*. Barrie & Jenkins, 1976.

McLean, Teresa. *Medieval English Gardens*. Collins, 1981.

Plumptre, George. *The Garden Makers*. Pavilion, 1993.

Scott-James, Anne. *The Cottage Garden*. Allen Lane, 1981.

Strong, Roy. *The Renaissance Garden in England*. Thames & Hudson, 1979.

Stroud, Dorothy. *Capability Brown*. Country Life, 1950; Faber, 1975.

Stroud, Dorothy. *Humphry Repton*. Country Life, 1962.

Stuart, David. *The Kitchen Garden*. Hale, 1984.

Symes, Michael. *The English Rococo Garden*. Shire, 1991.

Symes, Michael. *A Glossary of Garden History*. Shire, 1993.

Symes, Michael. *Garden Sculpture*. Shire, 1996.

Tait, A. A. *The Landscape Garden in Scotland, 1736-1835*. Edinburgh University Press, 1980.

Taylor, Christopher. *The Archaeology of Gardens*. Shire, reprinted 1988.

Thacker, Christopher. *The History of Gardens*. Croom Helm, 1979.
Thacker, Christopher. *The Genius of Gardening*. Weidenfeld & Nicolson, 1994.
Thomas, Graham Stuart (editor). *Recreating the Period Garden*. Collins, 1984.
Verey, Rosemary. *Classic Garden Design: How to Adapt and Recreate Garden Features of the Past*. Viking, 1984.
Watkin, David. *The English Vision: the Picturesque in Architecture, Landscape and Garden Design*. Murray, 1982.
Whittle, Elisabeth. *The Historic Gardens of Wales*. HMSO, 1992.
Williamson, Tom. *Polite Landscapes, Gardens and Society in Eighteenth-century England*. Alan Sutton, 1995.
Willis, Peter. *Charles Bridgeman and the English Landscape Garden*. Zwemmer, 1977.

There are numerous guides to individual gardens. Among surveys of British gardens in general are:

Gapper, Frances and Patience, and Drury, Sally. *Blue Guide to Gardens of England*. Black, 1991.
Hellyer, Arthur. *The Shell Guide to Gardens*. Heinemann, 1977.
Holles, Sarah, and Moore, Derry. *The Shell Guide to Gardens of England and Wales*. Deutsch, 1989.
Plumtre, George. *Collins Book of British Gardens*. Collins, 1985.
Rose, Graham, and King, Peter. *The Good Gardens Guide*. Vermilion, annual.

More detailed descriptions of individual gardens will be found in volumes of *The Gardens of Britain* series, edited by John Sales (Batsford, 1977-9):

1. Patrick M. Synge. *Devon and Cornwall*. 1977.
2. Allen Paterson. *Dorset, Hampshire and the Isle of Wight*. 1978.
3. Richard Bisgrove. *Berkshire, Oxfordshire, Buckinghamshire, Bedfordshire and Hertfordshire*. 1978.
4. Tom Wright. *Kent, East and West Sussex and Surrey*. 1978.
5. Kenneth Lemmon. *Yorkshire and Humberside*. 1978.
6. John Anthony. *Derbyshire, Leicestershire, Lincolnshire, Northamptonshire and Nottinghamshire*. 1979.

Related volumes to the series are:

Sales, John. *West Country Gardens: Gardens of Gloucestershire, Avon, Somerset and Wiltshire*. Alan Sutton, 1980.
Sidwell, Ron. *West Midland Gardens: Gardens of Hereford and Worcester, Shropshire, Staffordshire, Warwickshire and West Midlands*. Alan Sutton, 1981.
Verney, Peter. *The Gardens of Scotland*. Batsford, undated.

THE GARDEN HISTORY SOCIETY

The Society was founded in 1965 to bring together those interested in garden history in its various aspects: garden and landscape design and their relation to architecture, art, literature, philosophy and society; plant introduction, propagation and taxonomy; estate and woodland planning and maintenance; and other related subjects. The Society works to ensure the conservation of parks and gardens of historic interest and the adoption of historically valid methods of restoration and management. The journal of the society, *Garden History,* is published twice a year and members also receive a *Newsletter* three times a year. Visits and tours to parks and gardens of historic interest throughout Britain and overseas are arranged for members and there is an active Scottish group. Details of membership may be obtained from the Director, The Garden History Society, 77 Cowcross Street, London EC1M 6BP.

72. Design for 'A Parterre of Imbroidery of a very new design' from 'The Theory and Practice of Gardening', a translation by John James of a work by Alexander Le Blond, published in 1728.

Index

Page numbers in italic refer to illustrations.